TO THE STARS:

*KANSAS POETS OF THE
AD ASTRA POETRY PROJECT*

EDITED AND WITH COMMENTARY
BY
DENISE LOW

DISCUSSION GUIDE
BY
CARYN MIRRIAM-GOLDBERG

Center for Kansas Studies of Washburn University
Mammoth Publications

© 2009 Denise Low, commentary
© 2009 Caryn Mirriam-Goldberg, discussion guide

All copyrights for individual poems remain with the poets or their representatives.

ISBN 978-0-9800102-7-5

Published by
Center for Kansas Studies of Washburn University, Topeka
Mammoth Publications, Lawrence

Distributed by Mammoth Publications
1916 Stratford Rd., Lawrence, KS 66044

Available online through mammothpubs@hotmail.com and
www.mammothpublications.com

Cover painting and design by Paul Hotvedt

AD ASTRA PER ASPERA:

To the Stars through Difficulties

INTRODUCTION

This book collects the online flyers, or one-page "broadsides," that I distributed as poet laureate of Kansas 2007-2009. I began the biweekly project with the idea of alternating between historic and contemporary Kansas poets, but as the weeks went on, I found so many living poets that I shifted focus to emphasize their accomplishments. From their works, I chose poems that had some regional focus.

I have missed many fine poets, which I regret. I look forward to continuing recognition of poets through more Ad Astra broadsides.

Guidelines for inclusion in this project are: substantial connection to the state; and at least one poetry book published by a literary press. Many of the writers in these pages also have poetry-centered educations and careers, including national and state-level awards. These poets edit literary magazines, teach writing in correctional institutions, work with children, curate reading series, run conferences, lead library discussion groups, conduct residencies with senior citizens, and teach poetry to cancer survivors, victims of domestic violence, hearing impaired people, and residents of low-income housing. My wish is to make Kansas citizens aware of activities that nourish spirit and intellect.

As poet laureate, I came to appreciate more fully how much poetry is an aspect of the most accomplished literacy. Understanding literal denotations is an aspect of the reading process, but understanding the suggested implications makes reading (and listening) a complex reflective process that can include logic, emotion, and spirit.

I appreciate the efforts of many individuals and organizations that support this project: Washburn University and the Washburn Center for Kansas Studies; Thomas Fox Averill, friend, nominator, and supporter; Blue Heron typesetters and Paul Hotvedt, painter and collaborator; Jonathan Holden and Caryn Mirriam-Goldberg, fellow poets laureate and great friends; the Kansas Arts Commission and its remarkable staff and board, who sponsor the Poet Laureate program; 2007-2009 Kansas governors Kathleen Sibelius and Mark Parkinson; Greg German, who developed the Kansas poets website; Imagination & Place Committee, Raven Bookstore, Oread Bookstore, the University of Kansas English Department (where I was visiting professor for part of this project), Lawrence Arts Center; many kind friends; all these poets who commit their talents and lives to an essential art; Grandmother Carrie Strittmatter Dotson and Great-Aunt Hazel Bruner, who were early Kansas poets; and Thomas Pecore Weso, who makes possible many adventures.

Denise Low, 2009

JAMES LANGSTON MERCER HUGHES (1902-1967)

Langston Hughes was born in Joplin and raised in Lawrence until 1915-16. He maintained lifelong friendships with Lawrence classmates, teachers, and family friends. He was a true genius: he innovated the art of mixing spoken words with music, still an evolving American art form. He celebrated African American culture as he wrote poetry using the conversational vocabulary and sometimes in blues rhythms. He was a leader of the Harlem Renaissance in New York City, where he wrote plays, performed poetry, and mentored writers. He was a journalist, essayist, novelist, lyricist, and children's author.

When my husband and I researched Hughes's life in Lawrence for our book *Langston Hughes in Lawrence*, we found his homes were within walking distance of the Kaw River. He must have walked to its banks and watched the incessant current. The Kaw indeed is a "muddy" river that can be "golden" at dusk.

In this poem, Hughes calls on his memory of rivers as he catalogues, or lists, rivers important to world civilizations. He writes in uneven lines but maintains the poetic feel by using parallel beginnings and repetitions. He wrote of his poetry that it was often "racial in theme" and in "the rhythms of jazz." This free-flowing poem could be an improvised solo.

Education: Langston Hughes attended grade school and junior high in Lawrence, Kansas, graduated from high school in Cleveland, attended Columbia University, and earned a B.A. in 1929 from Lincoln University, a historically black university. **Career:** Beginning with the book of poetry *The Weary Blues* (Alfred A. Knopf 1926), Hughes made his living as a professional writer and lecturer. He published over 40 books and wrote numerous plays. In addition to leaving over a dozen poetic works, Hughes wrote prose as well, including: *Simple Speaks His Mind, Simple Stakes a Claim, Simple Takes a Wife,* and *Simple's Uncle Sam.* He edited the anthologies *The Poetry of the Negro* and *The Book of Negro Folklore* and wrote an acclaimed autobiography, partly set in Kansas, *The Big Sea.* His novel *Not Without Laughter,* set in Kansas, also is based on his life.

THE NEGRO SPEAKS OF RIVERS

I've known rivers:
I've known rivers ancient as the world and older than the
flow of human blood in human veins.

My soul has grown deep like the rivers.

I bathed in the Euphrates when dawns were young.
I built my hut near the Congo and it lulled me to sleep.
I looked upon the Nile and raised the pyramids above it.
I heard the singing of the Mississippi when Abe Lincoln
went down to New Orleans, and I've seen its muddy
bosom turn all golden in the sunset.

I've known rivers:
Ancient, dusky rivers.

My soul has grown deep like the rivers.

© 1959 Harold Ober Assoc. Inc., "The Negro Speaks of Rivers." Portrait by Winold Reiss

GORDON PARKS (1912 - 2006)

Gordon Parks, a native of Ft. Scott, Kansas, is best known as a photographer and filmmaker, but he also wrote books of poetry. In an interview he claimed he liked writing poetry best, but making a living directed his energies to other fields. Like Parks, many arts practitioners find writing poetry helps them to learn techniques that transfer to other uses. Parks was adept at screenwriting, fiction, memoir, essays, and narrative photography as well as poetry.

The poem "The Funeral" shows Parks' ability to compress a story into a few strong images. Homecoming is an archetypal situation, like the biblical Prodigal Son's return. With three imaginative—or "leaping" (to use Robert Bly's term)— comparisons, the poet shows the shift from childhood perspective to adulthood. The "mountains," "raging rivers," and "wide roads" the narrator knew as a boy have become "hills," "streams," and "a crooked path of dust."

Like a sonnet, this poem pivots near the end, turning from the landscape to the true drama of mortality. The narrator contemplates not only his childhood home, but also the final home, a resting place in a cemetery. The depiction of his father as a "giant" and the weight of the coffin imply a larger story about character. The mythic father kept his exaggerated status to both the child and the man who narrates. This appears to be an autobiographical poem, but even when the facts and intent are autobiographical, the artifice of verse makes the narrator into a somewhat fictionalized character who speaks directly to readers through carefully chosen words.

Education: Gordon Parks attended public schools in Ft. Scott, Kansas, and Minneapolis. **Career:** Parks' writing credits include the autobiographical *The Learning Tree* (1963). Collections of poetry (some with photographs) are: *A Poet and His Camera* (Viking 1968), *Whispers of Intimate Things* (Viking 1971), *In Love* (Lippincott 1971), *Moments Without Proper Names* (Viking 1975), *Arias of Silence* (Bulfinch Press 1994), *Glimpses Toward Infinity* (Little, Brown 1996), *A Star for Noon: An Homage to Women in Images, Poetry and Music* (Bulfinch 2000), *Eyes with Winged Thoughts* (Atria 2006). The Gordon Parks Center site is http://gordonparkscenter.org/

THE FUNERAL

After many snows I was home again.
Time had whittled down to mere hills the great mountains
of my childhood.
Raging rivers I once swam trickled now like gentle streams
and the wide road curving on to China or Kansas City
or perhaps Calcutta
had withered to a crooked path of dust
ending abruptly at the county burial ground.
Only the giant that was my father remained the same.
A hundred strong men strained beneath his coffin
when they bore him to his grave.

© 2008 Gordon Parks Foundation "The Funeral." © 2004 Bill Snead photograph

WLLIAM EDGAR STAFFORD (1914-1993)

William Stafford is my first choice for the exemplary Kansas poet. He spent his life in Kansas up to World War II, and Kansas is ever present in his writings. His verse exhibits the language, values, and experience of the Great Plains. He describes the sky's drama: its Milky Way swirls, wind-churned clouds, and limitless space. His poems also pay attention to the expansive earth below sky: its animals, plants, peoples, and histories. When I met Stafford we shared stories about childhood rambles along edges of town—creeks and pastures—and how these influenced us as adults. His words take us on extended outdoors walks.

However, Stafford does more than describe landscape; rather, he shows it is a stage for human inquiry into the nature of existence. His poems are riddles. Each asks questions about not just the human condition, but about the condition of the cosmos itself. He was a person of great faith, yet his poems are not preachy. He leads us to a hillside to ponder with him, and his inquiry becomes a tool of belief.

This poem begins at the edge of a town, where civilization becomes subject to time's passing. Look for shifts in Stafford's poems or pivotal words, such as "but" and "sage" in this poem. At the end, the poem shifts to the point of view of the sage, which appears to "flash" or wave to the onlooker. And notice the balance of the last line, both the "Yes" and the suggestion for "no."

Education: William Stafford, born in Hutchinson, graduated from Liberal High School and received a B.A. (1933) and M.A. (1947) from the University of Kansas. He received a Ph.D. from the University of Iowa (1954). **Career:** Stafford taught at Lewis and Clark College 1948 to 1980. Until his death he traveled widely speaking about poetry and writing. He won a National Book Award (1963) for *Traveling Through the Dark*. In 1970 Stafford was Consultant in Poetry to the Library of Congress, now the U.S. Poet Laureate position. He was poet laureate of Oregon.

FOR A DISTANT FRIEND

Where Western towns end nobody cares,
finished things thrown around,
prairie grass into old cars, a lost race
reported by tumbleweed.

And hints for us all stand there, small
or shadowed. You can watch
the land by the hour, what hawks overlook,
little things, grain of sand.

But when the right hour steps over the hills
all of the sage flashes at once,
a gesture for miles to reach every friend:
Yes. Though there's wind in the world.

© 1990 William Stafford Family "For a Distant Friend," *Kansas Poems of William Stafford* (Woodley Memorial Press) © 2007 Steven Hind photograph

JACK DeWERFF (1924 -)

Jack DeWerff is a published cowboy poet from the Ellinwood area. The cattle industry remains strong in Kansas, and this very American art form also still thrives. Its origins go back to the 1870s cattle drives from Texas to Kansas. In 1985 the first cowboy poetry conference started in Elko, Nevada. Most often cowboy poetry is about the trail, ranching, and Western life adventures. Cowboy poetry is essentially storytelling that can be set to tunes—hymns, sea chanties, or ballads. Because this verse fits patterns of familiar songs, the rhyme and meter are important. These also help memory. Jim Hoy's book *Prairie Poetry* is further introduction to this popular style. DeWerff has presented his writings in anthologies, spoken word compilations, and cowboy poetry gatherings.

"Married to a Cowboy" refers to the cruder aspects of a cowboy life—fondness for chewing tobacco and lack of personal hygiene. Like most cowboy poems, it is a long narrative, so this is an excerpt. DeWerff's narrator disarms his listener with self-deprecating humor—he anticipates criticisms and admits to them. The rhymes also create a humorous mood. This is a typical Kansas ploy to smooth relationships, and here a husband attempts to placate a wife. He also asserts the golden qualities of the cowboy character—honesty and loyalty.

Education: Jack DeWerff graduated from Ellinwood High School and learned ranching as a boy. **Career:** Jack DeWerff and his wife Loretta (Tedford) DeWerff farmed south of Ellinwood until 1975, when he began working for the Kansas State Animal Health Department. In 1990 he published a book inspired by his rodeo experiences, *Cowboy Philosophy in Rhyme* (Ellinwood). His is included in the audio CD *Echoes of the Trail* and other compilations. He has performed his verse at Western gatherings for cowboy traditions. He has been heard on national and regional radio programs.

from MARRIED TO A COWBOY

It ain't easy being married to a cowboy;
It takes the patience of Job, I am sure.
They come in dirty, and wet,
And smell like horse sweat,
And track in lots of mud and manure.

And they ain't worth a hoot doing housework,
Like cleaning or makin' the bed.
And sometimes she wishes
He'd help with the dishes,
But he'll go strum his guitar instead.

Etiquette ain't in his vocabulary;
He spits in a cup when he chews.
And at a dinner affair,
If two forks are there,
He won't know which one to use….

He forgets anniversaries and birthdays,
And sometimes he'll scratch where it itches.
But his word is good,
He wouldn't cheat you if he could.
And his friends mean more to him than riches….

© 1990 "Married to a Cowboy," Jack DeWerff, *Cowboy Philosophy in Rhyme*. © 2009 Kevin D. Hendricks, photograph

THOMAS ZVI WILSON (1931 -)

One of the most beloved poets in the Kansas City-Lawrence area is Thomas Zvi Wilson. He and his wife, poet Jeanie Wilson, have lived in Shawnee since 1992. Tom Wilson mentored a generation of area poets through editorial dialogues He also has supported the Kansas City Writers Place as a board member. Like Wilson, most poets work within a community or educational group in order to craft their writings into the best possible form. Perhaps this collaboration of poets is particular to the genre. Poetry is a communal art, even when print-based and not oral.

Wilson's background as a visual artist is evident in the structures of his writing. He collages layers of images onto a canvas and then reworks them until each shows clearly. He also balances the outer details of a scene with inner reflection, and he understands how light plays over the entire scenario of a painting or a poem.

In "Klieg Lights," the narrator, a man similar to Wilson himself, watches the sun rise from his porch. This is an early summer poem, when sunrise comes sooner each day. The poet, however, conflates the sun with Klieg lights, which are bright carbon-arc lights used to illuminate movie sets. Artists also use such lights in painting studios, and so the poem seems to be a still life. Neighbors remain "nailed" to mattresses—so are passive to nature. Even the wind seems to be humanized, as it does not even snore. Then comes the true action of the poem: penance. The narrator counts his "sins" and hopes for forgiveness. He sees his yard as a "stony patch of garden" not too distant from Eden. He describes this peaceful moment and stresses his audit of "pleasures," like volunteer weeds.

Education: Thomas Zvi Wilson was born and educated in New York City and moved to Kansas when he was fifty (1981). **Career:** Wilson is a painter and sculptor with work in 25 museum and university collections. Wilson's books are *Deliberate and Accidental Acts* (BookMark Press 1996), runner up for the Thorpe Menn Award; and *The Door into the Dream*, with Jeanie Wilson (Mid-America Press 2006), a *Kansas City Star* Notable Book (2006).

KLIEG LIGHTS

Moon surrenders so sun may rise earlier,
turn on its Klieg lights while neighbors
are still in pajamas or robes, nailed
to their mattresses.
The wind is asleep, not even snoring.

I count my sins on the porch,
in cushioned silence and solitude,
audit my pleasures, pray that
in the end, though undeserved,
I'll be forgiven, and mercy will
be sprinkled on me like volunteer
weeds on this stony patch of
garden and this pleasant peace.

© 2006 Thomas Zvi Wilson "Klieg Lights," *The Door into the Dream* (Mid-America Press)
© 2002 Denise Low photograph

WILLIAM C. KLOEFKORN (1932 -)

In 1972, Windflower Press published William Kloefkorn's first book *Alvin Turner as Farmer*, which became a regional best seller. The publisher, Ted Kooser, later became U.S. Poet Laureate, and Kloefkorn became lifetime state poet for Nebraska in 1982.

Kloefkorn was raised in Kansas and has spent his career in Nebraska. Kloefkorn's verse, written in vernacular language, celebrates Great Plains life. He is one of the writers, along with Kooser, Harley Elliott, and others, to define a Midwestern voice. He often writes about rural life with understated wit and choice details. Kloefkorn is especially a storyteller. He also is one of the funniest poets. He has the ability to satirize some of the beloved practices of Midwestern folk, even the religion.

In this poem about Kansas religious icon Carry Nation, he tells history from a young person's point of view. Contrasts invigorate the story: the "full-fleshed" photograph breaks the wallpaper pattern. Mrs. Wilma Hunt sermonizes about morality as she destroys life. The devil appears, but then is set aside for Kool-Aid. The young observer remains fascinated with the final result—curled, dead worms.

The poet's dead-pan delivery suggests a presence in the poem besides Mrs. Hunt, Carrie Nation and the child: the open-eared listener/poet who observes, judges a tad, and chuckles at the absurd human condition. This could be the adult narrator, and it could be the reader.

Education: William Kloefkorn, was born in Attica, Kansas. He received a B.A. (1954) in English from Emporia State University and then served in the U.S. Marines. In 1956 he taught high school in Ellinwood, then returned to Emporia State University for the M.A. in English (1958).
Career: Nebraska named Kloefkorn the State Poet, the equivalent of state poet laureate. He taught at Wichita State from 1958-1962 and Nebraska Wesleyan University from 1962 to 1997. He is active as a writer and performer of poetry. His books—over two dozen—include poetry, fiction, memoir, fiction, and children's literature. His selected poems are in *Tree House: New & Selected Poems* (White Pine Press 1996).

LTL

Carry A. Nation came into our house and filled it
With her meagerness. She was hung full-fleshed
Against the flowered wallpaper of our living-room,
And Mrs. Wilma Hunt, who brought her, gave each
Of us a little wooden hatchet. "John Barleycorn
Is the Devil," Mrs. Wilma Hunt said. And
by dropping worms head-
First into alcohol she taught us
To hate him. "Now let me tell
You," she said, "about the LTL...."

She taught us the Loyal
Temperance Legion song, all of it, then killed
Another worm and served refreshments. Our house
Had never been so full. There were all of us, with
Carry on the wall-
Paper: Kool-Aid, Cookies, Song,
Something-New-to-Hate
And several dead worms
Curled in alcohol

© 1974 William C. Kloefkorn, "LTL." © 2009 Jim Reese photograph.

JO McDOUGALL (1935 -)

Jo McDougall was born and raised in Arkansas, where she received an M.F.A. under the legendary teacher and editor Miller Williams. She was director of the creative writing program at Pittsburg State University 1987-1998, and currently she resides in Leawood, Kansas.

McDougall brings a Southern sensibility to her writings about the great open Kansas landscape—her work is more narrative, perhaps, and her humor is direct. But the influence of the grasslands is strong in her spare language, use of sharp visual images, and themes of endurance. She is a committed realist. Some of her poems, for me, recall Grant Wood's paintings like "American Gothic," but with humor. Time creates a vivid dimension within McDougall's Midwestern settings, through the agent of memory. McDougall writes: "Memory is the poet's calico landscape of the imagination, recalled from the advantage of maturity." In her poetry appear flashbacks, obsessive replays, time travel, sustained observations, and reflections. Ironically, McDougall's pragmatic insights construct a personal and even spiritual view of the cosmos.

In "Blessing," McDougall creates a story with selected details. The Kansas setting is alluded to with the presence of wind, storm, and sun. The small town intimacy with neighbors is suggested by the narrator's nosiness. How long was the narrator watching in order to see all these details, including hidden panties? The last line opens the scene to the point of view of the narrator—who is also participating in the scene. It is her "ritual."

Education: Jo McDougall graduated from DeWitt High School. She received an A.A. from Stephens College, B.A. from University of Arkansas (1957) and an M.F.A. in Creative Writing from the University of Arkansas-Fayetteville (1985). **Career:** This poet has published *Satisfied with Havoc*, (Autumn House 2004); *Dirt* (Autumn House 2001); *From Darkening Porches* (University of Arkansas 1996); *Towns Facing Railroads* (University of Arkansas 1991); *The Woman in the Next Booth* (BookMark-University of Missouri-Kansas City 1987); and *Women Who Marry Houses* (chapbook, Coyote Love, 1983). Her work has been adapted for film (*Emerson County Shaping Dream*), theater, music, and artist's book. Inquiries about the film or books can be directed to her website: www.jomcdougall.net.

BLESSING

My neighbor hangs out the morning wash
and a storm dances up.
She strips the line,
the children's pajamas with the purple ducks,
her husband's shorts,
the panties she had hidden under a sheet.
When the sun comes out
she comes back
with the panties and the sheets, the shorts and the pajamas.
This is my ritual, not hers.
May her husband never stop drinking and buy her a dryer.

© 1991 Jo McDougall, "Blessings," *Towns Facing Railroads* (University of Arkansas Press)

CHARLES PLYMELL (1935 -)

Charlie Plymell was born in Holcomb during the Depression. He has written that his father was an Oklahoma cowboy, of Wyandot heritage, and his mother was of "Plains Indian descent." He was an early rebel against the status quo—as a high school student he dropped out and began traveling the country. He participated in the 1960s beat movement in Wichita, Los Angeles, San Francisco, and New York. Among the writers and artists he buddied with are Michael McClure, Bruce Conner, S. Clay Wilson, William Burroughs, and Lawrence Ferlinghetti. Since 1974 he has edited and published Cherry Valley Editions in New York. He regularly visits family and friends in Kansas. He has an online presence: and continues to be an active writer and performer of his poetry.

Plymell celebrates details of geographic places in many of his poems, whether Paris, Utah, Baltimore, or Nueva York. Like many Kansans, he is an inveterate traveler, and he has some of the best highway poems. "Not a Regular Kansas Sermon" references Kansas culture in several ways: the subsistence living, with pear cactus and jackrabbits making a meal; and a faith that makes psychological survival possible. This poem recapitulates the Depression and the Trail of Tears—both historic events that shaped this region. He has a declamatory style, with the ability to compress stories to their barest, most gleaming bones. Many of his poems are extended narratives, and this is a selection from one of these.

Education: Charles Plymell attended North High School in Wichita and Wichita State University. He received an M.A. in creative writing (Johns Hopkins 1970). **Career:** Dave Haselwood published Plymell's first poetry book, *Apocalypse Rose* (San Francisco 1966), and Lawrence Ferlinghetti published his novel *The Last of the Moccasins* (1971). His other dozen books include *Forever Wider, 1954-1984* (Scarecrow 1985), *Was Poe Afraid* (Bogg 1990) *Hand on the Doorknob* (2000), and others listed online: http://www.cherryvalleyeditions.com , as well as books he has edited. The University of Delaware collects his manuscripts and papers.

from NOT A REGULAR KANSAS SERMON
For my mother in the hospital

Your grandmother married out of
the Trail of Tears.
You were born to a trail of fears,
a soddy, your brother dead.
Now you mistake me for him.

Then came the dust storms.
You put wet wash rags
over our faces so we could breathe.

Many women went mad, "God's Wrath"
in the storms, miles from anywhere.
It took strength, courage and prayer.
You shot jackrabbits to feed five kids
and even fed hoboes from the tracks.

You gathered cactus for us to eat.
(I saw some at a gourmet market in D.C.)
I've yet to see snow ice cream
or mayonnaise & sugar sandwiches.
I did see fry bread recently
at Harbor Place in Baltimore. . . .

© 1985 Charles Plymell, "Not a Regular Kansas Sermon"

KENNETH LEE IRBY (1936 -)

Ken Irby is a Kansas poet who practices projective verse, a form based on physical acts of speechmaking rather than British poetics. Charles Olson of Black Mountain College (1930s-1950s) taught that a line should be the length of a breath. In poetry like Irby's, the words match human consciousness rather than creating a facsimile of reality. This "open field" style may suggest prose of William Faulkner or James Joyce more than Shakespeare's sonnets. Irby was not a student at Black Mountain, but he has had contacts with Black Mountain poets throughout his career. This direction in American writing connects to experimental forms loosely called "Language" poetry.

Poet Ed Dorn was a student of Olson and close friend of Irby. In this elegy, Irby displaces emotional grief for Dorn with an image of farm animals in a bare pasture. The season is near solstice, the darkest, most mysterious time of year, and also a time when losses are most sharply seen.

The poem begins with the animals viewed at a distance, as though they are almost beyond sight. The narrator sees them skewed by the distance—and also perhaps by grief—so that they appear to be performing on hind legs, "a real dog and pony show." Irby sets this familiar term amongst the more bizarre appearances of the domestic animals. Just when it seems he might explain himself and the soundless "musicians at the window," he changes direction. He shifts from visual images to sounds—the rhyme between "cray" and "they." The second section also shifts from animals to plants: "hedge apples" (or osage oranges) at pasture boundary and "night winter cray bushes." Rather than resolve the poem with a resounding click, he opens to new questions.

Education: Kenneth Irby, born in Texas, was raised in Ft. Scott, Kansas. He received an A.M. from Harvard University and M.L.S. from the University of California-Berkeley. **Career:** Irby is an English professor at the University of Kansas, and he has been a Visiting Professor at the University of Copenhagen. His books are *The Intent On: Collected Poems 1962-2006* (North Atlantic 2009), *Studies* (First Intensity 2001), *Ridge to Ridge* (Other Wind 2001), *Call Steps* (Station Hill 1992), *A Set* (Tansy 1983), *Orexis* (Station Hill 1981), *Catalpa* (Tansy 1972), and *To Max Douglas* (Tansy 1971).

[For Ed Dorn –2 Apr 1929 – 10 Dec 1999]

in the far back pasture animals have lined up in lament
dog goat pony horse and beyond them
a cow in its astronomical agility
a real dog and pony show
giving tribute back on their hind legs
musicians at the window
lacking the cock his call
the show of the world

along the fence rows in with the hedge apples
the night winter cray bushes are in bloom.
the cray? what are they?
that is their rhyme

© 2001 Kenneth Irby "[For Ed Dorn]" from *Studies: Cuts, Shots Takes* . © 2007 Denise Low photograph

GLORIA VANDO (1936 -)

Gloria Vando Hickok has enriched the Kansas City area literary community since moving to Johnson County in 1980. She founded *Helicon Nine*, a nationally recognized women's arts magazine, which then became a press, Helicon Nine Editions. In addition, she and her husband Bill Hickok co-founded The Writers Place, a literary arts center in Kansas City. This poet combines such service with writing award-winning books.

Vando is a Nuyorican: a person of Puerto Rican heritage born in New York City. She layers this cultural perspective through her verses. Most of her poems begin with autobiographical moments, which then expand into global perspectives. Narrative is a strong element in all of Vando's works, and also history. She regales her readers with dramatic stories set in Sarajevo, Vietnam, Korea, San Juan, New York, and Kansas City. She personalizes political comment by adding emotional reactions to factual events. She also tells her own larger-than-life stories in well wrought verse.

"Orphans" is one of these stories. The fourteen-line poem follows an unrhymed sonnet pattern. The first eight lines set up the situation—death of a loveless parent—and then the poem shifts to the mother's advice about grief. Acorns and wind are familiar images to Midwestern readers, and here these natural forces suggest wholeness. The last two lines are the sonnet's couplet, with the surprising final chord—acceptance of "luck." The mother empowers her orphaned (or fatherless) daughter by framing her within a larger cosmos.

Education: Gloria Vando received a B.A. from Texas A and I College and pursued graduate studies at Southampton College, Long Island. **Career:** Vando's *Promesas: Geography of the Impossible* (1993) was a Walt Whitman finalist and won the Thorpe Menn Book Award. *Shadows and Supposes* (2002) won the Poetry Society of America's Alice Fay Di Castagnola Award and was Best Poetry Book of 2003 (Latino Hall of Fame). She has received the Kansas Governors Arts Award and an Editors Grant from the Coordinating Council of Literary Magazines.

ORPHANS

When my father died, leaving me
distraught for never having known
him as father, as friend,
for never having known myself

as child of one whose eyes and mouth
and temperament were mine, my mother
cautioned me, told me not to mourn
what I perceived as loss: you and I

are daughters of the wind, she said,
you and I are fathers of our souls,
sprouting intact like seedlings
from two wind-borne acorns.

We thrive on luck, she said,
there is no father's love in that.

© 1993 "Orphans," Gloria Vando, *Promesas* (Arte Público Press)

VICTOR CONTOSKI (1936 -)

My first college teacher of poetry was Victor Contoski, a professor at the University of Kansas. He encouraged his students unconditionally; he instructed; he insisted we purchase copies of literary magazines and imagine ourselves in their pages; and he encouraged us to learn how to write reviews. Contoski also taught his students to read Midwestern writers closely, especially William Stafford, Robert Bly, and Ted Kooser. He imparted a sense of excitement about creating a literature for a part of the country that is often overlooked by outsiders.

Contoski's *noir* writing is a contrast to his classroom geniality. His deep imagist poetry creates a stage for dark post-World War II ironies. He was greatly influenced by his Polish wife's experiences during the war and his own experiences teaching in Poland during the Cold War. Absurdist humor underlies the outlook of survivors, and this humor seeps through Contoski's works.

Contoski himself writes haunting, vivid and unsettling poems about rain, stars, frontier history, and myths. "Sunset" is set during a somber time of day. Its setting, the Western frontier, is a backdrop for Spanish horsemen, nursery rhymes, and western cowboy heroes who die. Finally, the European folklore figure Jack enters into the grasslands landscape, reincarnated as a Wild Man figure, and now at home in a cottonwood tree as well as a beanstalk. And the final victor is nature itself, the constantly moving sun. Midwesterners are survivors of a harsh frontier history and a harsh environment.

Education: Victor Contoski grew up in Minneapolis He received a B.A. in Ancient Greek and M.A. in English (University of Minneapolis); and a Ph.D. in American literature (University of Wisconsin 1969). **Career:** 1961-1964 he lived in Poland, where he lectured in American literature and was a Fulbright professor. He taught at the University of Kansas from 1969 to 2007 and won the HOPE teaching award. His books of poetry are *Astronomers, Madonnas, and Prophesies* (Northeast/Juniper Books 1972); *Broken Treaties* (New Rivers Press 1973); *Names* (New Rivers Press 1973); *A Kansas Sequence* (Tellus/Cottonwood Review Press 1983); *Midwestern Buildings: A Collection of Poems* (Cottonwood Press 1997); and *Homecoming* (New Rivers Press 2000). He also has edited and translated Polish-related writings.

SUNSET

Since long before the white man
rode out onto the prairies
the sun has been going down.

A towering cottonwood sways in the breeze
rocking rocking the cradle in its branches.

The hero's eyes turn glassy.
His hand waves vaguely
toward something in his breast
as his knees buckle.

The giant coming down the beanstalk
feels it start to sway beneath him.

He looks down and sees Jack
with a silly grin and a hatchet
looming suddenly larger and larger

as the sun over Kansas
goes down and down and out.

© 2000 "Sunset" by Victor Contoski, *Homecoming* (New Rivers Press).

ELIZABETH AVERY SCHULTZ (1936 -)

Elizabeth Schultz, of Lawrence, combines enthusiasm for art and nature in her writings. As a literature professor at the University of Kansas, she encouraged thousands of students to examine stories closely and then to link observation with reflection. She brings that sense of joyful scrutiny to her creative writings, which include essays and poetry. Often she links these to nature. Since retirement in 2001, she has continued to be active as a Fulbright scholar, poet, and ecocritic activist. She is a member of the Committee on Imagination & Place and consultant to its press; she also writes for the Nature Conservancy and other organizations.

Schultz delights in patterns, whether crafted by natural processes or artisans. She engages deeply with both, as seen in this poem. A great blue heron's carcass has an unexpectedly beautiful form. The poet compares it to a macramé dream catcher; crochet-work; an amulet; and also its vertebrae are frets of a guitar. As insects scour its bones, this erasure creates yet another pattern. Forces of the river that sustained the living bird cause its final dissolution. So the poet humanizes an emblem of mortality—the skeleton. The most descriptive words and phrases of the poem are set like gems along strands of short lines, so that "dark amulet," "polished blade," and "shining insects," along with other terms, resound fully. The poem shows paradox in uncovering aesthetic joy in river refuse. The title is also paradoxical: Does this mostly decayed beast, lodged on a sandbar, tell about life on the Kansas River? Indeed, the river does shape the living forms of river birds like this heron, especially the long legs for wading.

Education: Elizabeth Schultz received a B.A. in European History (Wellesley 1958), and M.A.(1962) and Ph.D. (1967) in English from the University of Michigan. She taught at the University of Kansas 1967-2001. **Career:** Schultz is the author of *Unpainted to the Last: Moby-Dick and Twentieth Century American Art* (University Press of Kansas 1995); a memoir, *Shoreline: Seasons at the Lake* (Michigan St. U. Press 2001); *Conversations: Art Into Poetry at the Spencer Museum of Art* (2006); *Her Voice*, poems (Woodley Press 2008); The *White-Skin Deer: Hoopa Stories* (Mammoth 2009), fiction; and essays in *The Nature of Kansas Lands* (University Press of Kansas 2009).

WATCHING THE KANSAS RIVER

On a sandbar
a heron is laid
out with care.
A dream catcher,
its design is
pressed into sand.
Its wings stretch
in skeletal symmetry.
Feathers crochet
its light bones.
Its feet curl into
dark amulets,
and its beak is
a polished blade.
Scarabs bead
its intricate fretwork.
Relentlessly,
remorselessly,
the shining insects
devour the design,
releasing the bird
into a river of light.

© 2009 Elizabeth Schultz "Watching the Kansas River" published on Friends of the Kaw website http://www.kansasriver.org/content/schultz_profile

HARLEY ELLIOTT (1940 -)

Harley Elliott is the Kansas poet's poet. He is the writer I studied to learn the best ways to write about grasslands and inner landscapes of the imagination. I also studied how his words flow as smoothly as conversations among friends. He uses an unassuming mid-Plains dialect—peppered with vivid images. I consider him the first English-language poet to use fully this region's vernacular in poetry. Elliott also writes longer works about history of the West, as well as whimsical and surreal poems. *Loading the Stone* (Woodley 2006) is a unique prose work that straddles fiction and nonfiction. He has had career opportunities to leave Salina, yet he remains in his hometown.

Elliott's writing reflects his attachment to prairie spaces. He eschews labels. He told an interviewer: "I was really conscious that if I wasn't careful I would get put into this box called 'prairie poet.'" This poem is directly about avoiding the stereotypes of labels. He suggests all words can limit direct experience of reality. He tries to overcome the "slippage" or imprecision of language and also its limitations—"the danger of names."

In this case, the monarch butterfly walks on his face, and "blinded by words," he fails to match its "shining light." Elliott's "hinged mosaic" description for butterfly wings here is one of my favorites. He addresses his readers and asks us to join in his quandary about how to express relationship with nature. In this poems resolution, the sky creature and earthly narrator "rush together" in union.

Education: Harley Elliott graduated from Salina High School. He received a B.A. from Kansas Wesleyan University and an M.A. in art from New Mexico Highlands University. **Career:** This poet and artist spent four years in Syracuse, New York, after college, where he established relationships with New York publishers, including Dick Lourie (Hanging Loose Press). He returned to Salina and taught art at Marymount College until it closed. Then he worked in arts education at the Salina Art Center. His ten books of poetry are from Crossing Press, Hanging Loose, Juniper, Woodley Press (Washburn University), and others. They include *Darkness at Each Elbow* (Hanging Loose Press 1981); *The Monkey of Mulberry Pass* (Woodley 1991).

BUTTERFLY MASTER

This butterfly stopping on my cheek
would choose yours too
if you had fallen down among
grass and pasture flowers
and your face closed
hard as mine.

This small hinged mosaic
of orange black and palomino
has been given a name
and the danger of names hovers
close to both of us today.
Walking up it stops at
the doorway of my eye:
there I am
blinded by words
in the shining light of its face.

We rush together
earth and sky.

© 1993 Harley Elliott, "Butterfly Master." © 1989 Denise Low, photograph

ROBERT DAY (1941 -)

Robert Day is best known as a masterful prose writer. His novel *Last Cattle Drive* is a classic of contemporary American frontier literature. Less well known is the fact that Day received his M.F.A. from the University of Arkansas in poetry writing. The grace of his style indicates serious study of language. Whether he writes essays, articles, novellas, or poetry, he understands aesthetics of style—balance, invention, and timing.

Day's verse zings. He compresses scenes into their vital parts, sets up ironies, then, in the last lines, turns to readers and unveils a startling revelation.

In "Teal Hunting with Two Old Uncles," the setting of season and place is clear. The poem's speaker has an easy assurance, inviting readers into his low-key drama. This youthful narrator contrasts with older uncles, as he performs the heavy work of sodding the duck blind. The early autumn day reflects the uncles' mellow old age concerns of storytelling and casual drinking. For them, their weapon of choice is a "rolled up" magazine. They create their own oral history compendium, a parallel to the magazine, as the young hunter goes about business. Years later, like the uncles, the narrator remembers exactly what he shot on that trip, the "Blue wings" and "Cinnamon." With his uncles, he becomes like "old hunting dogs loaded with dreams," not so concerned with the hunt for meat as for the distillation of memories into fine narratives.

Education: Robert Day received his B.A. and M.A. degrees in English (University of Kansas 1964, 1966) and M.F.A (University of Arkansas-Fayetteville 1970). **Career:** Day has published poetry: *We Should Have Come by Water* (Mammoth 2009) and prose: *The Committee to Save the World* (Western Books 2009), *Speaking French in Kansas* (Cottonwood Press 1989), and *The Last Cattle Drive* (Putnam 1977). He taught at Fort Hays State University, Washington College in Chestertown, Iowa Writers Workshop, University of Kansas, and Montaigne College, The University of Bordeaux. He has won awards from Pen Faulkner/NEA, Pushcart, and National Endowment for the Arts. He is past president of Associated Writers and Writing Programs.

TEAL HUNTING WITH TWO OLD UNCLES

September's never cold enough for ducks and whiskey.
I shoot in Tee-shirt and moccasins
as green wings hustle from pond to pond
in the yellow morning.

My uncles miss chances, drinking
on the bench deep in the blind
swapping stories about Cheyenne Bottoms
and Snow Geese bigger than the moon.

In the afternoon I work shirtless, laying
strips of sod on the blind's roof,
careful as my mother tiling her kitchen counter.
My uncles sit on campstools whacking at wasps
with rolled up *Ducks Unlimited*.

That evening I shot two limits: Blue wings
came in low over the decoys. I dropped
a lone Cinnamon at sundown. My uncles
napped on their bench, twitching.

Like old hunting dogs loaded with dreams.

© 2009 Robert Day "Teal Hunting with Two Old Uncles," *We Should Have Come by Water* (Mammoth)

DIANE GLANCY (1941 -)

Diane Glancy, of Prairie Village, has German, English and Cherokee heritage. She grew up in Kansas City, where she learned paradoxes of urban Native life. She writes about her family, American Indian histories and the Midwest. Her novel *Pushing the Bear* is one of the best-known accounts of the *Tsalagi* (Cherokee) Trail of Tears. Her novel *Stone Heart* is about Sacajawea. She has been a role model for many Native writers, and she is one of the most prolific writers from Kansas.

Glancy often blends experimental forms with strong storytelling elements. "Indian Summer," for example, tells the story of a farm breakup, but also it suggests the season's changes alongside historic changes. The image of a tool set broken apart suggests the displacements when a farm family leaves the land. The reference to an American Indian dress suggests the earlier historic diaspora of Native peoples. Glancy uses a pastiche of images to suggest the process of time.

The images—farmhouse, leaves, bugs, cornfields, dress, tools and barn--appear on a fictitious country road. The narrator drives by them and sees an "open sea" and finally the "white iceberg" barn. The barn's isolation is highlighted by the comparison to ice, and also the narrator is alone within time. Nonetheless, spirits remain in the garden, and all times exist at once. Nothing completely ends.

Education: Diane Glancy has a B.A. in English, University of Missouri (1964); M.A., Central State University (1983); M.F.A., University of Iowa Writers Workshop (1988). **Career:** Diane Glancy has written more than 20 books of poetry and more than 20 books of prose; plus a number of plays produced and published. Collected poems are in *Rooms: New and Selected Poems* (Salt Publishing, EarthWorks Series, Cambridge, England, 2005). She was a professor of English at Macalester College until 2009. She has won awards from the National Endowment for the Arts, the National Endowment for the Humanities, the Lannan Foundation, Wordcraft Circle of Native Writers and Storytellers, and many others. She is also a filmmaker, working from her original scripts.

INDIAN SUMMER

There's a farm auction up the road.
Wind has its bid in for the leaves.
Already bugs flurry the headlights
between cornfields at night.
If this world were permanent,
I could dance full as the squaw dress
on the clothesline.
I would not see winter
in the square of white yard-light on the wall.
But something tugs at me.
The world is at a loss and I am part of it
migrating daily.
Everything is up for grabs
like a box of farm tools broken open.
I hear the spirits often in the garden
and along the shore of corn.
I know this place is not mine.
I hear them up the road again.
This world is a horizon, an open sea.
Behind the house, the white iceberg of the barn.

© 2007 Diane Glancy, "Indian Summer," *Asylum in the Grasslands* (University of Arizona Press). © 2005 Denise Low, photograph.

JONATHAN HOLDEN (1941 -)

Jonathan Holden, first Kansas poet laureate, has lived in Manhattan, Kansas, since 1978. He is distinguished professor at Kansas State University. I first met Holden when I taught at K-State briefly in the 1970s, and I observed how he was generous to many poets and students. At that time Scott Cairn studied under him and others. He has influenced the direction of American poetry—through essays, teaching, and example—by insisting that informal, domestic moments are high art.

Holden is passionate about poetry, both as critic and poem-maker. His brilliance manifests in his performances as well as writings. He can quote entire poems by major American and British poets for hours. He masters fields of knowledge—mathematics, tennis, U.S. politics, Bach—and finds ways to use them in everyday situations.

This poem, about apparently ordinary sights, comments upon instinctive knowledge. It mimics the perfect balance that both baseball players and sparrows must practice in order to survive. The lines shift in rhythm, to imitate how birds totter and regain stability. Holden uses a passel of rich descriptive verbs, like "pirouette" and "stab," to describe reflexive movements of the birds and players. These contrast to hesitations—reflection and philosophy—in the poem. Instinct keeps us alive, especially in the infield, where quick reactions are survival.

Education: Jonathan Holden grew up in rural Morristown, New Jersey, described in his memoirs *Guns & Boyhood in America* and *Mama's Boys*. His college degrees, all in English, are from Oberlin (BA 1963), San Francisco State College (MA 1970), and University of Colorado (PhD 1974). **Career:** This poet has published twenty books of poetry, essays, memoirs, and a novel. *Knowing* is his most current book of poetry (University of Arkansas Press 2000). He is poet-in-residence and University Distinguished Professor at Kansas State University. He has won awards from the National Arts Endowment, University of Missouri Press, the Associated Writing Programs, and others. Midwest Quarterly devoted the summer 2007 issue to him. His website is www.jonathanholden.com.

NIGHT GAME

These infielders are definite
as sparrows at work.
Split that seed with one peck
or starve.
There is no minor league
for birds. There is
exactly one way
to pirouette into a double play
perfectly. The birds
don't dare reflect on what
they do, each hop, each stab and
scramble through the air into the
catch of the sycamore's
top twigs
is a necessity,
absolute. To stay alive
out in the field, you must be
an authority on parabolas
and fear philosophy.

© 1997 Jonathan Holden "Night Game," *Ur-Math,* State Street Press

MICHAEL L. JOHNSON (1941 -)

Michael L. Johnson, a longtime poet, also lectures and writes about the American West. He has been a professor at the University of Kansas since 1969, teaching creative writing and literature. His prose book about the western frontier, one of the best on the subject, is *Hunger for the Wild*. He also publishes prose and poetry about art, culture, and many other topics. Johnson writes eloquently in the genre of poetry about the cultural history of this region. Since he was born in next-door Missouri, he knows this small-town life well through experience, and he does painstaking research. Few people realize how deeply creative writers research their subjects for accuracy and telling details. Johnson's verse exemplifies this.

Hunting is one of this region's traditions, and "Hunting Again" is a terse sketch about the stalking process, written as though readers were in the field with the narrator. The rhythmic pace is regular and efficient. Discomfort of the expedition is noted in details—the "heft" of the gun; the prick of "burrs" and the "clutch of underbrush."

But Johnson does not leave readers with a single, flat image. In the second stanza, he digs more deeply into the experience. As the hunter seeks to take another being's life, he also confronts his own mortality, his own "uncertain ghost." He confronts a memory "so deep," which is the underlying nature of humankind: We are predators, and this poem does not make apologies for this survival skill.

Education: Michael L. Johnson received his B.A. from Rice University (English 1965); M.A. from Stanford University (English 1967), and Ph.D. from Rice University (English 1968). **Career:** He has published seven books of poetry: *From Hell to Jackson Hole: A Poetic History of the American West* (Bridge House Books 2001, Ben Franklin Award from the Publishers Marketing Association), *Violence and Grace: Poems about the American West* (Cottonwood Press 1993), *Ecphrases* (Woodley Press 1989), *Familiar Stranger* (Flowerpot Mountain Press 1983), *The Unicorn Captured* (Cottonwood Review Press 1980), and *Dry Season* (Cottonwood Review Press 1977). He has published over a thousand poems in *Westview, California Quarterly, Illinois Quarterly, Northeast Journal, Portland* Review, and others.

HUNTING AGAIN
for Pete

Things are different out here,
our ears tuned for a flush,
eyes set for scat or tracks.
Our soft hands heft oiled steel,
part branches, pluck off burrs.
Our legs ache from mud's tug,
rough clutch of underbrush.
Our noses trust the dog's
to discover the ghosts
of birds, where they are or
only where they might be.

We remember so deep
having done this before:
in the stalk, in the quick
moments of violence,
we discover ourselves,
our own uncertain ghosts.

© 2001 Michael L. Johnson "Hunting Again," *From Hell to Jackson Hole*

JAMES O. McCRARY (1941 -)

James McCrary first came to Lawrence in 1965 and mostly has lived in Kansas since, except for short spans on the coasts. In the sixties he was an active poet associated with Ed Dorn, David Ignatow, Ken Irby, and John Moritz, with publications in *Grist* magazine. In 1990 he began teaching poetry at the Lawrence Arts Center and curated several reading series, including the Poetry Slam. He also worked with Burroughs Communications.

McCrary writes a minimalist verse that follows thought so closely that it becomes an abstraction. His writings have much in common with abstract paintings. John Fowler writes of this poet that "the simplicity of language, the sparseness of the word on the page, the way a few words stretched my mind across big spaces, all this is here." McCrary's years in Kansas have marked his language, as poet Charlie Plymell notes that this poet's style resembles "a Kansan who doesn't want to waste any words." This minimal approach creates emphasis.

McCrary's writings are like gesture drawings of artists, where ink outlines horizons and encloses balloons of space. The first line of this poem, "7/25/91," sets up the philosophical framework, questions about "out there." Then the words suggest the very basics of thunderclouds gathering: clouds, movement, "electric," "a bit of wet," and more movement. Then the narrator compares weather to thought, which is "there" and "here" at once or "t(here)."

Education: Jim McCrary received a B.A. in English (1987) and an M.A. in Creative Writing (1989), under David Bromige. Both degrees are from California State University-Sonoma. **Career:** The poet has five books of poetry: *Coon Creek* (Cottonwood Books 1970), *Edible Pets*, (Tansy Books 1987), *West of Mass* (Tansy Books 1991), and *All That* (ManyPenny Books 2008 http://www.lulu.com/content/4363355). He has published a half dozen chapbooks and has poems in over 100 magazines, anthologies, and online venues, including *Exquisite Corpse, Caliban*, and *First Intensity*. He edits his own 'zine *Smelt Money*, a print-version blog. He received a Phoenix Award from the Lawrence Arts Commission.

7/25/91

Thinking about out there
the clouds gather
push east and south
to here
where hopefully they will
do what they do
covering both sun and land
with the mass of them

some electric
some noise
a bit of wet
then move on toward the
easy hills of west missouri
or simply dissipate and
reflect above the kansas river
where the loss is obvious

not much else is t(here)

© 1994 James McCrary, "7/25/91," *Poems of the Place* (Grist)

B. H. FAIRCHILD (1942 -)

One of the most successful poets from Kansas is Pete Fairchild. He grew up in Liberal, Kansas, the far southwestern, high plains edge of the state. Early mapmakers once labeled this region the Great American Desert. His poetry evokes the isolated small-town landscape, including Main Street buildings and the wild edges of town. He also conjures the emotional landscape of those who dream and survive the arid Great Plains. Here, a literary imagination is not a frill, but rather a tool of endurance. Fairchild mythologizes Kansas by enlarging it in his personal memory. Also, he shows how European traditions lie alongside those of mid-continent America. He is a complex American poet, with the ability to mix history, popular culture, observation, and stories.

Fairchild's "desert" is a busy crossroads. In another poem, "The Big Bands: Liberal, Kansas, the Summer of 1955," the poet explains how swing bands toured the region after their popularity faded elsewhere.

The poem "Hearing Parker the First Time," about Charlie Parker, shows how radio airwaves also cross this flyover region. Fairchild uses some less familiar language: "Eleusinian mysteries" are ecstatic Greek rites. He refers to Coleman Hawkins and Lester Young, who are saxophone players with ties to Kansas and Kansas City. And "Ornithology" is the title of one of Parker's albums (he was known as Bird). The poet pays homage to jazz as a less successful musician who first learned to play the saxophone and then the instrument of the American language.

Education: B.H. Fairchild, born in Houston, attended Liberal, Kansas, public schools and the University of Kansas (M.A. in English 1968). His Ph.D. is from the University of Tulsa (1973). **Career:** Fairchild's books of poetry are *Early Memory Systems of the Lower Midwest* (National Book Critics Circle Award, Norton 2003); *Local Knowledge* (Quarterly Review of Literature 1991); *The Art of the Lathe* (Alice James 1998); and *The Arrival of the Future* (Swallow's Tale 1985). He taught at California State University-San Bernardino from 1976 to 2005. He has won numerous honors.

HEARING PARKER THE FIRST TIME

The blue notes spiraling up from the transistor radio
tuned to WNOE, New Orleans, lifted me out of bed
in Seward County, Kansas, where the plains wind riffed
telephone wires in tones less strange than the bird songs

of Charlie Parker. I played high school tenor sax the way,
I thought, Coleman Hawkins and Lester Young might have
if they were, like me, untalented and white, but Ornithology
came winding up from the dark delta of blues and Dixieland

into my room on the treeless and hymn-ridden high plains
like a dust devil spinning me into the Eleusinian mysteries
of the jazz gods though later I would learn that his long
apprenticeship in Kansas City and an eremite's devotion

to the hard rule of craft gave him the hands that held
the reins of the white horse that carried him to New York
and 52nd Street, farther from wheat fields and dry creek beds
than I would ever travel, and then carried him away.

© 2003 B.H. Fairchild, "Hearing Parker the First Time," *Early Occult Memory Systems of the Lower Midwest,* W.W. Norton © 2007 Denise Low, photograph.

WILLIAM J. HARRIS (1942 -)

Billy Joe Harris, University of Kansas professor, spent a sabbatical year studying poets and painters, including the artist Giorgio Morandi. He told an interviewer that he admires Morandi for "muted colors and radically reduced subject matter." He employs this approach to his own verse. His work suggests narratives, but in such concise form that cultural referents may be minimal. Structures of poems are visible and directly reflect the subjects.

In the poem "Sympathetic Magpies," the Chinese origin of the legend is secondary to the universal concept of bridges. Further, the stanzas' own parallel lines suggest intervals of bridge girders.

In the poem, love creates a bridge between mortal and immortal beings, and the interplay between heaven and earth are universal. The memorable magic here is the bridge made of magpies. So far the poem has parable-like simplicity, with love that can defy the decrees of heaven. Like bridges, romance between a young weaver and herder can be set in most times and places. The Milky Way itself is another kind of bridge.

Then Harris shifts to present time, inviting readers to also become part of legends through the poem. With a few simple images—lovers, Heaven, and bridges—the poet creates a story, briefly outlined yet complete like a Morandi painting. Harris said of the painter: "His quiet visual drama tells you that you need no more than these few objects to tell the human story."

Education: Harris received a B.A. in English (Central State University 1968), M.A. in Creative Writing (Stanford University 1971), and Ph.D. in English and American Literature (Stanford University 1974). **Career:** This poet and critic's book publications are *Hey Fella Would You Mind Holding This Piano a Moment* (Ithaca House 1974), *In My Own Dark Way* (Ithaca House 1977), and *Personal Questions* (forthcoming from Leconte Publishers, Rome). He has published in over fifty anthologies, including *Every Goodbye Ain't Gone* (The University of Alabama Press 2006) and *The Body Beautiful* (Henry Holt 2002). He is the author of the critical work *The Poetry and Poetics of Amiri Baraka: The Jazz Aesthetic* (University of Missouri Press 1985) and editor of *The Leroi Jones/Amiri Baraka Reader* (Thunder's Mouth Press, 1991 2000).

SYMPATHETIC MAGPIES

There is an old Chinese legend
About a weaving girl and a cowherd
Falling in love and being punished
By Heaven because she was celestial
And he was a mere mortal

Heaven only allowed them to meet
Once a year
On the seventh day
Of the seventh month

The magpies were so sympathetic
Each year
On that day
They made themselves
Into a bridge
Stretching across the Milky Way
So the lovers could kiss

Poems are sympathetic magpies
Bridges between lovers
Bridges between selves
Bridges between worlds

© 2009 William J. Harris "Sympathetic Magpies"

STEVEN A. HIND (1943-)

For over twenty-five years, Steven Hind has published poetry about life in the Great Plains and Flint Hills of Kansas, including the small towns. Robert Frost is an influence, as well as fellow Kansas poet William Stafford. Hind's language appears simple, and his people are salt of the earth. Tragedy, extreme weather, and economic disasters complicate the rural experience. Nonetheless, Hind also celebrates the vivid natural life of the region, where animals may be as distinctive as next door neighbors. "Blue Heron" is an example of Hind's sensibility.

Many Kansans are avid bird watchers, whether formal members of the Audubon Society or just roadside observers. Hundreds of bird species migrate through the mid-continent skies, and many remain as year-round residents. Great blue herons are colorful water birds found along river banks and marshy areas. The poet accurately acknowledges the bird's habitat, which is "Behind the pond."

Hind shows how poetry involves research and observation. This poem could be a simple snapshot of the bird—until I look more closely at Hind's language and see how he enlivens the description with comparisons. Nearly every line challenges me to see two images at once: willows sound like a silk scarf unfurling; the heron lowers and raises its head like a jackknife closing and opening; guitar frets appear on the water; and the great bird's wings are like oars of a rowboat. The ending line, "the bright gravel of stars," is an inversion, where earth and sky reverse positions, echoing the poem's theme. This dizzying image shows the possibilities for language to surprise and delight.

Education: Steven Hind was born and raised near Madison, in the Flint Hills. He earned a B.A. from Emporia State University and an M.A. in English (1970) from the University of Kansas. **Career:** Hind taught at Hutchinson Community College and Topeka High School for 36 years. His books are *Familiar Ground* (Cottonwood Review Press 1980); *That Trick of Silence* (Washburn 1990); *In A Place with No Map* (Washburn 1997); and *Loose Change of Wonder* (Washburn 2006, Kansas Notable Book Award). His CD *Waking in the Flint Hills* is available by writing to 503 Monterey Way, Hutchinson, KS 67502.

GREAT BLUE HERON

Behind the pond under a whispering
scarf of willows, heron does his lone
knifewalk beside the wind-fretted waters.
His deft movements make a death
defying progress: a life of mud transmuted
into sky life as he rows away on a river
of air and its melody of coyote song
through cedars beyond cedars, their
silhouettes swallowed by darkness
beneath the bright gravel of stars.

© 2006 Steven Hind "Great Blue Heron," *Loose Change of Wonder*

PHILIP MILLER (1943 -)

This poet has been a mainstay of the Kansas City poetry scene, where he co-founded the Riverfront Reading Series. He served on the editorial boards of Woodley, Potpourri, and BookMark Presses and on the boards of The Kansas City Artists Coalition and The Kansas City Writers Place. He co-edited (with Carl Bettis) the magazine *The Same* (2000-2007), for which he is the current editor. He is also contributing editor to the online magazine *Big City Lit*. After retiring from teaching creative writing, he moved to Mount Union, Pennsylvania.

His poetry is chock-full of surprising language and philosophical twists. "Like a Tree" is a poem I have tried to write many times, without this poet's success. Miller compares his body at length to a tree with the idea that human organic forms are like other natural forms—hair is like "leaves"; digits are like "twigs"; and lungs have bronchial alveoli like "sponges." This breaks down the separation of body and mind, expounded in the philosophy of René Descartes. Miller posits reality as a unified field, where thought is a natural process, like gravity. Humans and trees both are mortal and eventually will fall.

The poem shifts into high gear with the description of the head, which includes "inner petals" where he connects "what our brains conceive" to the physical voice. The poet's words are organic constructions, "unwrapped and uttered by way of bone and blood." Miller shows how even the most common poetic subject, a tree, can be renewed by placing it within new context.

Education: Philip Miller attended public schools in Kansas City, Kansas. He received a B.A. (English and Psychology 1965) and M.A. (English 1966) from Emporia State University. **Career:** Miller taught English at Kansas City Kansas Community College (1986-2002). His books are: *Cats in the House* (Woodley Memorial Press 1987); *Hard Freeze* (BookMark-University of Missouri-Kansas City 1994); *From the Temperate Zone* (with Keith Denniston, Potpourri Press 1995); *Branches Snapping* (Helicon Nine Editions 2003); *Why We Love Our Cats and Dogs* (with Patricia Lawson, Unholy Day Press 2004); *The Casablanca Fan* (Unholy Day Press, forthcoming). He won the Ledge Press chapbook award (1995).

LIKE A TREE

The body owns us, lets us, inside it, live
and breathe through branchy sponges it provides:
the head covered with hairs like leaves,
the trunk's limbs sprouted
with fingers and toes like twigs,
and within, the heartwood's dark thuds
are the ax man's steps, which will bring it down,
this body with a head like a bloom,
and with inner petals, too, delicately tissued
purses and pods of sap and seed,
and the Adam's apple, the vocal chords and tongue
give us a voice which is the body's voice,
full-throated, words of the flesh,
unwrapped and uttered by way of bone and blood.
Only by the always-bodily thing are we
brought to what our brains conceive
before the body falls like a tree.

© 2003 Philip Miller, "Like a Tree," *Branches Snapping* (Helicon Nine Editions) © 2001
Denise Low photograph

JAMES VINCENT TATE (1943 -)

James Tate grew up in Kansas City, on both sides of the state line, and he attended Pittsburg State University. He then went to Iowa University, which launched his distinguished career as a poet known for his "dream logic." The laws of the imagination, in his poems, are as potent as laws of physics. He is able to draw readers into his vision by telegraphing vivid images that are suggestive of stories. This allows readers to invest their own experiences into the accumulated information. His technique is like Aesop's fables, which strip stories to their basic elements. His plot sequence, however, is more subtle.

"Late Harvest" is one of Tate's few regional poems. He seldom attaches his imagination to finite geography. In this poem he collages together colorful images: "white buffalo," "red gates," dried out "cellophane" grasses, and a "black tractor." What he captures is specific to this geography: the distorted size of late afternoon sun, as it stretches into the horizon. Dimensions in the grasslands have greater depth, so objects may line up as though they were visionary. The "white buffalo" may be drained of color by the sun-glare optics, it may be albino, or it may be a spiritual being—or all of these things. The narrator is surprised by the buffalo, but he cannot rouse the birds nor the girls, who accept this cosmos. The falling of night quiets his fears, as natural order returns. In this poem Tate shows Kansas as a mythic place.

Education: James Tate received a B.A. in English (Pittsburg State University 1965) and an M.F.A. in Creative Writing at the University of Iowa Writers' Workshop (1967). **Career:** Tate is distinguished university professor at the University of Massachusetts-Amherst. His second book, *The Lost Pilot* (Yale University Press 1967), won the Yale Series of Younger Poets. His *Selected Poems* (1991) won the Pulitzer Prize and the William Carlos Williams Award, and his *Worshipful Company of Fletchers* (1994) won the National Book Award. In 2001, he was elected a Chancellor of the Academy of American Poets. He has published over a dozen books of poetry and prose.

LATE HARVEST

I look up and see
a white buffalo
emerging from the
enormous red gates
of a cattle truck
lumbering into
the mouth of the sun.
The prairie chickens
do not seem to fear
me; neither do the
girls in cellophane
fields, near me, hear me
changing the flat tire
on my black tractor.
I consider screaming
to them; then, night comes.

© 1991 James Tate, "Late Harvest," *Selected Poems*. © 2007 Star Black, Academy of American Poets, photograph.

STEPHEN E. MEATS (1944 -)

Stephen Meats was born in LeRoy, Kansas, and raised in Concordia. One of his contributions to Kansas literary culture is his service as poetry editor of *Midwest Quarterly*. In that role he has curated special issues of regional poetry, including one devoted to the first Kansas poet laureate Jonathan Holden. He is able to fulfill this poet's poet role because of his own fine verse. His book *Looking for the Pale Eagle* is a rare poetry best seller—the first printing sold out quickly.

Meats writes poems that often begin with the commonplace. Concrete details make his work accessible to any reader, yet his works have complex layers of image and motion. He sets his poems in specific places like a storyteller, but his poems have lyrical intent—they end with emotion.

This recent poem, "My Advice," gives directions for enjoying the countryside of Kansas. Meats describes a typical prairie road that is not spectacular, yet small, substantial joys unfold. Perhaps this is a road like Robert Frost's roads, one less traveled by. He suggests that his readers stop and collect "chat," or roadbed gravel, to reposition at home. The reflective moment of collection is when sky, birds, and landscape are noticed. The rock is for remembering that moment. It is like a worry stone carried in the reader's pocket and touched often. The stone also suggests the folk tale about stone soup: after everyone contributes vegetables to a miraculous recipe, the original stone can be discarded. As a catalyst, its purpose is fulfilled. Poems are like such stones.

Education: Stephen Meats attended Kansas State University for three years before transferring to the University of South Carolina, where he earned his bachelor's (1966), master's (1968), and doctoral degrees in English (1972).
Career: Meats is University Professor and English Department Chair of Pittsburg State University. Since 1985, he has been poetry editor of *The Midwest Quarterly*. Meats has published *Looking for the Pale Eagle* (Woodley Press, 1993). His poetry, articles, and fiction appear in *Kansas Quarterly*, *The Little Balkans Review*, *Albatross*, *The Quarterly*, *The Laurel Review*, *Blue Unicorn*, *Tampa Review*, *Arete*, *Hurakan*, *Flint Hills Review*, *Prairie Poetry*, *Dos Passos Review*, and others.

MY ADVICE

You say you want to find yourself. You'll need
a piece of gravel. Drive any rocked road
in Kansas and you'll hear pieces by the dozen

knocking in your wheel wells. For once, stop
and get out of the car. Take a minute to look
at the sky—flat bottomed clouds shadowing

the pastures. You'll hear the meadowlark
on the fence post before you see him fly.
Pick up your piece of gravel. If you're far

off the main route, a handful of chat, or even
road sand will do. Cup it in your palm while your
tires hum away the miles on the asphalt highway.

Warm it in your pocket as you drink your coffee
at the café counter in the next town, and stay
a while to look at the faces and listen to the talk.

Then take it home with you and right away
put it in your garden or your flower box or drop
it in the driveway. It doesn't really matter.
You've already got your answer.

©2008 "My Advice," Stephen Meats, in *Dos Passos Review*

PATRICIA TRAXLER (1944 -)

Writing is Patricia Traxler's life. Besides being a fine, fine poet herself, she has developed writing programs for the hearing-impaired, for seniors, for victims of domestic violence, and for mental health and stroke patients. Also, she founded the Salina poetry reading series. To all of these tasks, she brings the skills of a well-schooled, sophisticated versifier. She studied with Nobel winner Seamus Heaney, and she has national book publications. However, in an interview, Traxler avers that her "most important and rewarding work" is with disenfranchised populations. She grew up in San Diego, and since the late 1970s, she has lived in her grandparents' house in Salina.

Reading Traxler's work is like having intimate conversations with a narrator much like herself. She draws on her own Irish Catholic—and also Native—background, as well as her perspective as a woman. Her poems are spare stories that sometimes include romantic details. Often, she animates poems with the drama of relationships.

In "Why She Waits," the sky and the earth are husband and wife. Their tension arises from anticipation. Despite the "plain and faithful" landscape of late winter, even the drab and common starlings understand that renewal is about to occur. The "nightly" return of sky to earth is not a vivid kindling of male and female, but rather a routine of their relationship. Amidst this humdrum scene, however, a larger drama will unfold as snow melts into soil, and a new season is about to begin. The entire poem answers the title question about the "wife's" patience, why she is willing to wait.

Education: Patricia Traxler attended schools in California. She completed studies for the B.A. from San Diego State University. She studied at Radcliffe College as a Bunting post-doctoral fellow. **Career:** Traxler's books include: *Blood Calendar* (Morrow 1975); *The Glass Woman* (Hanging Loose 1983); *Forbidden Words* (University of Missouri 1994); and the novel *Blood* (St. Martin's Press, 2001/02). She has been poet-in-residence at the Thurber House (Ohio), Hugo Poet at the University of Montana, and a Kansas Arts Commission fellow.

WHY SHE WAITS

Another night: late winter falling
on the prairie like a nightly husband
no longer impassioned but knowing his rights
and duties

The snow no longer quite conceals
what for months has gone
unnoticed: the land, plain
and faithful beneath it
holding out

for something no one can describe, something
the starlings whisper about, evenings
in the melting snow, something
they look for
in the cold winter grass.

© 1983. Patricia Traxler, "Why She Waits ," Hanging Loose Press. 1986 William Stafford photograph

JEANINE HATHAWAY (1945 -)

Jeanine Hathaway teaches writing and literature at Wichita State University. Originally from Chicago, she settled in Wichita over thirty years ago. In her writings, she explores the intersections between knowledge and belief. She was a Dominican nun as a young woman, and these experiences also inform her work. Keen observation grounds her poems, which create situations for exploration of faith.

"Reconnaissance," a title that is also a synonym for exploration, focuses on a woman who could be a neighbor "across the street." I suspect she could also be a guise of the poet herself. Scenes in Hathaway's poetry could be set in Wichita, but they are made more general, to fit experience of any reader. Here, the neighboring woman forays into dark morning, a time that should be sunrise, but instead she is immersed in a sightless dark that reveals only self. This is the spiritual seeker's quest.

The poet compares this woman to a fish, awake yet submerged in watery depths. Her heartbeat centers her own "atmosphere," in a pre-dawn and pre-creation setting. Yet in this dark place, she finds two things: body and "grace." Whether in an urban setting or a hermitage, these are what create the paradox of incarnation.

Education: Jeanine Hathaway earned a B.A. in English (Siena Heights College 1970) and an M.F.A. in Poetry (Bowling Green State University, 1973). **Career:** This poet published *The Self as Constellation: Poems* (University of North Texas Press 2002), which won the 2001 Vassar Miller Prize for Poetry. She also published an autobiographical novel, *Motherhouse* (Hyperion 1992). For twelve years, she wrote monthly personal essays for *The Wichita Times*. She has been published in numerous journals and anthologies, including *DoubleTake*, *The Georgia Review*, *The Greensboro Review*, *River Styx*, *The Ohio Review*, and *The Best Spiritual Writing*. She has taught at Wichita State University over 30 years and received the Wichita State University Regents' Award for Excellence in Teaching in 1993.

RECONNAISSANCE

Before dawn, before the first
hushed light causes her children
to stir, the woman across the street
rises, every morning, extending
her life backwards into night
as a fish sated at the surface
will dive deeper and darker
until even sight is a memory
floating off.

She is alert now, aware of
herself as out of proportion,
mirrored through water;
expansive, most reflective
and faithful, and still
surrounded, governed
by the immense heartbeat
of her own atmosphere,
the unsettling grace of morning
and her cold feet.

©2002 Jeanine Hathaway "Reconnaissance," *The Self as Constellation* (University of North Texas Press)

MICHAEL POAGE (1945 -)

Michael Poage has been a Kansan since 1985, when he began serving United Church of Christ congregations in Council Grove, Lawrence and Wichita. He has advanced degrees in both theology and creative writing. While a student at the University of Montana, he studied poetry with Richard Hugo and Madeline Defrees, one of the great teaching teams of the 20th century. He learned economy of words. This poet's work begins with commonplace moments that are synecdoches—parts representing the whole (as sunflowers represent Kansas prairies). Poage's poems resemble enfolded macramé knots made of simple twine. His words are familiar yet they evoke nature's possibly divine order.

"Pelagic" in this title means living in open waters, referring most often to birds. With this poem, then, Poage might refer to how prairies resemble large bodies of water. However, he turns the sky, not ripples of grass, into the ocean, with the bird "swimming in the air." The counterbalance is land, or "home's street." To extend the water comparison further, he then imagines the moon also moving within an oceanic sky. He suggests the moon is love, "beauty," and mystery—all universal associations. The "small bird" and the moon both share the same fate as humans: all are "condemned" to struggle in "the open sea." Home is the familiar, and the sky is the natural world with all its powerful, uncertain forces.

Education: Michael Poage has a B.A. (Westmont College, 1967); M.F.A. in Creative Writing (University of Montana 1973); and Master of Divinity (San Francisco Theological Seminary 1985.). **Career:** His books are *BORN*, (Black Stone Press 1975), *Handbook of Ornament* (Black Stone Press 1979), *The Gospel of Mary* (Woodley Press 1997), *god won't overlook us*, (Penthe 2001), and *Abundance* (219 Press 2004). He has taught at Friends University, Wichita State University, and the University of Latvia. He is pastor of Fairmont United Church of Christ, Congregational, in Wichita; some sermons are posted at http://www.fairmountucc.com/sermons.htm

PELAGIC

In the breath
of a hand
we saw a small bird
swimming in the air.
We returned
to home's street.

The moon
is a human back
caught again
in an act of passion
and condemned
with all its beauty
and common questions
to the open sea.

© 1997 Michael Poage, "Pelagic," *The Gospel of Mary* (Woodley) © 2004 Denise Low photograph

JUDITH ROITMAN (1945 -)

Judith Roitman has lived in Lawrence since 1978. Besides being active as a poet, she is professor of mathematics at the University of Kansas. She is Guiding Teacher at the Southwind Zen Center and an active member of the Jewish community in Lawrence. These multiple roles inform her writing. In addition, she founded the Big Tent Reading Series, which sponsors diverse Lawrence readers.
She contributes to online commentary about contemporary poetics like Ron Silliman's and Jonathan Mayhew's blogs. Clarity of vision is a hallmark of her writing, yet the logic is unreliable, as random events are the rule, not the exception.

"As a Leaf" is a poem about the uncertain motion of falling leaves, perhaps set in the autumn season. Here, focus is on each image, and not the expected connections among them. Readers must fill in stories, if there are any. This poem is also about perception itself, as real images are copied on our retinas ("Copy to copy") and "transformed" into human experience. I also find this poem to be about poetry itself, which is like "turning the wrong corner" and finding new ways to perceive reality. A lyrical image is "suspended wasp motion" as time itself continues to move forward like heartbeats and like the slow, floating wasp's flight. The ending thought, about the tension between immobility and action, resolves with the "& so on" of continuing creation as our galaxy continues to spread outward across the blue sky. This kind of poetry asks the reader to participate fully.

Education: Judith Roitman graduated from Bayside High School in New York City (1962); Sarah Lawrence College with a B.A. in English (1966); and University of California-Berkeley, Ph.D. (Mathematics, 1974). **Career:** Roitman has published poems various journals, including *First Intensity, Black Spring, Locus Point* (on the web), *Bird Dog*, and *Wakarusa Wetlands in Word & Image* (Lawrence: Imagination and Place, 2005). She has published these books: *The Stress of Meaning: Variations on a Line by Susan Howe* (Morris, Minn.: Standing Stones Press 1997); *Diamond Notebooks* (Buffalo: Nominative Press Collective 1998); *Slippge* (Elmwood, Conn.: Potes and Poets Press 1999); and *No Face: New and Selected Poems* (First Intensity 2008).

AS A LEAF

Copy to copy as a leaf falls transformer to transformed
light on glass moving as hands denied & flight

suspended from wings but without looking
all things against blue the blue room blue house

we find it this way every so often turning the wrong corner
the right one filling up all gone against blue

covered within light the heart the sign of it steady
the wire angling up into vision

things ready to fall
& others spinning up suspended wasp motion

within derelict acts & clarity of motion
stillness within motion & so on.

© 2008 Judith Roitman "As a Leaf" (First Intensity Press)

JOHN MORITZ (1946 – 2007)

John Moritz attended the University of Kansas during the late 1960s and remained in Lawrence the rest of his life. He founded Tansy Press and Tansy bookstore. Steve Bunch remembers: "With his 'Putpenny Pomes' you could put a penny in a jar and take away a small folded mimeographed poem." Moritz was no capitalist. Through his advocacy of cutting-edge poetry, he advanced the direction of American poetics. Among the writers he published are Ed Dorn, Kenneth Irby, Alice Notley, Paul Metcalf, Joanne Kyger, and Robin Blaser. In the 1980s he sponsored a poetry reading series that featured some of these authors, and a broadside for each.

Moritz promoted poetry in every possible way; he was himself a fine poet (I remember urging him to focus more on his own writing). Reviewer Richard Owens notes Moritz's connection to Black Mountain writers: "The writing leads back to [Charles] Olson via Dorn." Focus on natural flow of language itself rather than traditional forms is apparent in Moritz's work. Also, his verse has a lyrical, emotional tug. He attunes to place as well as to tradition.

The poem "Omaha" has almost no punctuation. It illustrates Moritz's concern with joining his imaginative impulse to solid reality. The poem begins as a journey through neighboring Nebraska, where he turns an urban scene, 12th Street, into a western overland trail. But this quest ends at a restaurant, not the Missouri River ("Big Mo"). He finds a gar, a trash fish, imprisoned in a decorative pond. Its displacement resonates with "meat packing plants"—what hunting has become within a city landscape. At the end, as Moritz turns his thoughts to poetry—Dante and Ezra Pound—he connects movement of consciousness to the gar's thrashing: all fight against confinement.

Education: John Moritz was born in Gary, Indiana, graduated from high school in Chicago (1964), and attended the University of Kansas. **Career:** Moritz was a poet, publisher, printer, and bookstore proprietor. Founded Tansy Press and worked in the printing business throughout his life. He published poems in *First Intensity, Skanky Possum, Black Rain, Damn The Caesars*, and *House Organ*. His recent books include: *Mayaland/Catfish Frenzy* (First Intensity Press 2007) and *Cartography* (First Intensity 2002).

OMAHA

The drive south on 12th is on an hispanic artery
pumped by the meatpacking plants
lots of mom and pop comidas
but we were questing
catfish at the end of the trail
while waiting to be seated
a gar circles a ceramic pond counterclockwise
in fresh water, clear enough to see the coins
tossed for an aimless wish, the gar circles
out of its water which would be the Big Mo sludge
fishermen who snag a gar reeling in their line
take out a vengeance with a knife or boot
but this particular gar circles and thrashes
like Dante's fornicators or late Pound
circling Language with one foot nailed to the floor.

© "Omaha," *Catfish Frenzy*, permission of Sharon Hoffman Moritz, 2007. © 2007 Sharon Moritz, photograph.

PATRICIA REEVES (1947 -)

Trish Reeves is committed to poetry. One of my favorite stories about her took place the evening of September 11, 2001. She continued with a previously scheduled poetry reading, despite the tragedy. After her presentation, a woman thanked her for commitment to the calling of poetry. In times of crisis, especially, poets speak for community. They express shared sorrows; they celebrate victories.

The intense, short lyric is this poet's forte, with attention to heart more than story. Reeves' work draws upon the European arts tradition, translated into Midwestern lifeways. This creates a tension, as Old World icons find places in American farmlands. In "Chronology" the poet refers to Van Gogh's suicide and his oil painting technique of layering paint on a canvas—*impasto*. His thick paint strokes are vivid and unsubtle—heightened with emotion. The poem resonates with the issue of farmers' suicides, too common and dramatic in the heartland as family farms lose economic viability.

The seasonal cycle of summer sowing and autumn harvesting in "Chronology" is replaced not by a calendar timeline, but by an emotional calendar. Reeves creates a new timekeeping paradigm here, suggested by Van Gogh and by farming, but instead based on more personal: anniversaries of family deaths. When I read this poem, I remember my ancient grandmother mourning her father's death anniversary, seventy years later., but the years had no relevance. Van Gogh's death also is a timeless event.

Education: Trish Reeves was born and educated in St. Joseph. She received her B.A. from the University of Missouri School of Journalism. She received an M.F.A. in Creative Writing, Warren Wilson College. **Career:** Her first book, *Returning the Question*, won the Cleveland State University Poetry Center Prize (1988). BookMark Press of UMKC published *In the Knees of the Gods: Poems* (2001). Her work is recognized by fellowships from the National Endowment for the Arts, the Kansas Arts Commission, and Yaddo; and she was a Keck Fellow at Sarah Lawrence College. She edited *New Letters Review of Books*. In 1991 Reeves became an English professor at Haskell Indian Nations University, Lawrence. She works with literary programs for the Johnson County prisons and Kansas Council for the Humanities.

CHRONOLOGY

"Goes out into the field
and shoots himself."
Well wouldn't you know
this is the guy we adore.
The wheat wild with him,
the crows crazed and we
so undecided
about life ourselves
that the least mention
of Arles and
self-portraits put on *impasto*
has us thumbing through
our pasts for the date
he entered them with his sorrow
as vividly as a death in the family
that links us to our
fate like the calendar
on which numbers are unnecessary.

© 2001 Trish Reeves "Chronology," *In the Knees of the Gods* (BookMark-University of Missouri-Kansas City Press) © 2009 New Letters photograph

LINDA LYNETTE RODRIGUEZ (1947 -)

Linda Rodriguez was born in Fowler, graduated from Manhattan High School, and attended Kansas State University before dropping out to hitch-hike to Haight Ashbury in the 1960s. Since 1970, she has lived in Kansas City, where she was director of the University of Missouri-KC Women's Center. Rodriguez is vice-president of the Latino Writers Collective, and she has published in numerous journals and anthologies, including *Primera Página: Poetry from the Latino Heartland*. Her new collection *Heart's Migration* won the Elvira Cordero Cisneros Award. She is of Western Cherokee descent.

In "Coyote Invades Your Dreams," Rodriguez reminds us of how psychologically close Kansans are to animal life. Coyotes stalk fringes of cities and pasturelands. Even in urban areas, coyotes—and cousin red foxes—create dens in roadside ditches and soccer fields. Their voices harmonize with car traffic and cicadas.

The adaptation of these wily beasts is instructive—we humans also learn environments quickly and well. We share animal qualities of stalking, shifting identities, and forming attachments. Here, a lover is a coyote-trickster who both attracts and frightens. The body is the narrator's "traitor," the human part that responds to the lover's temptation. Rodriguez uses this extended metaphor to explore the complexities of human romance. The lesson is: Any coyote encounter leaves its mark.

Education: Linda Rodriguez has a B.A. in English-Creative Writing/Journalism (University of Missouri-Kansas City) and an M.A. in English (University of Missouri-Kansas City). **Career:** She is the former Director of the UMKC Women's Center; and now she is a personal achievement coach, editor and freelance writer. Her poetry books are *Skin Hunger* (Potpourri Publications, one of *Writer's Digest's* four top poetry chapbooks of 1995) and *Heart's Migration* (Tia Chucha Press, 2009 Elvira Cordero Cisneros Award).

COYOTE INVADES YOUR DREAMS

You're staying clear
of him. Just because
you noticed him once
or twice doesn't mean you want
anything to do with him.
He's beneath you—
and above you and inside you
in your dreams. His mouth
drinks you deep, and you come
up empty and gasping
for air and for him. That traitor,
your body, clings to him like a life
raft in this hurricane
you're dreaming. His face
above yours loses its knowing
smile as he takes you. Again,
this night, you drown
in your own desire. Coyote
marks you as his.
You wake to the memory
of a growl.

© 2009 Linda Rodriguez "Coyote Invades Your Dreams," *Heart's Migration* (Tia Chucha 2009)

ALBERT GOLDBARTH (1948 -)

For more than twenty years, Albert Goldbarth has taught in Wichita State University's M.F.A. creative writing program. During that time he has won major prizes for his poetry and essays. Goldbarth is originally from Chicago, and he has not lost the urbanity of that place. He also brings a profound depth of language experience to his work. He studies cultural and historic texts and alludes to them freely. Intellectual thirst is a striking aspect of his writing—and another is his seemingly infinite vocabulary.

Goldbarth's longevity in the Kansas university system suggests compatibility with his adopted home. What he shares with his fellow Kansans, I believe, is self-deprecating humor. He pokes fun at all sorts of folks, but most especially himself. Second, he voices strong opinions, also like most Kansans. And he has no patience with phoniness. Thus earnestness underlies the poet's ironies and occasional sarcasms. Despite a harsh, realistic depiction of details, he affirms the ten-million myriad beings of this flawed world.

Like other Kansans who survive the extreme seasons, both physically and psychologically, Goldbarth is a person of faith. In "Wings" his narrator finds a bird carcass. Rather than describe a headless bird, the speaker conjures the image in human terms, specifically wings of a theatrical stage. But he speaks as though the stagehand were an executioner or *deus ex machina*. In the next section, and the poet marks the break with a line, he looks at the desiccated animal remains, but without the distance of metaphor. He accepts "hard summer; the land enameled." He accepts life disintegrating into dust. Then, like many Kansans, he finds solace in prayer.

Education: Albert Goldbarth received a B.A. from the University of Illinois (1969) and an M.F.A. from the University of Iowa (1971). He pursued further graduate studies at the University of Utah (1973-4). **Career:** Goldbarth's most recent book is *The Kitchen Skin: New and Selected Poems* (Greywolf Press). He has published over twenty books of poetry, four books of essays, and a novel. He has won two National Book Critics Circle Awards for poetry; a Guggenheim fellowship; three National Endowment for the Arts fellowships; and a PEN Center West Award.

WINGS

I always wondered why they called them wings.
—Perhaps because somebody always waited in shadow
in them, with a rope.
With a rope like a great braided nerve
and while some sweet singing or bloody melee
completely filled the central light, this person
would raise or lower the god.

It's summer. Hard summer; the land enameled.
I find the bird already half-dismantled
by ants—the front half. It's flying
steadily into the other world, so needs to be this still.
Do I mumble? yes. Do I actually pray? yes.
Yes, but not for the bird. When we love enough
people a bird is a rehearsal.

© 2007 Albert Goldbarth, " Wings," Greywolf Press © 2007 Denise Low, photograph

JEANIE WILSON (1948 -)

Jeanie (Olson) Wilson was born in Eureka, Kansas, in the Flint Hills. Her father's ancestors are Norwegian and settled in a community near Eureka called Lapland. Her great-great grandmother on her mother's side migrated to this area with nine children and settled on 500 acres. She farmed the land, where later oil was discovered. This immediate connection to region and history inform her writing, as well as the tradition of strong women. She has had an active life as a poet and curator of poetry readings, often in conjunction with her husband Thomas Zvi Wilson.

"The Screen Porch" is a mix of times, from present to past and back again. The first stanza sets the scene: she is on the porch of the family farm. Sounds are natural, and she, like the cicadas and bull frogs, is subject to natural "rhythms." What humans understand more than other species, though, is their mortality. The second stanza goes back five generations to the great-great grandmother—the famer and matriarch. Her life resumes on the porch for an instant, as she rests "from the day's heat," alongside the future voice of the poem's narrator. Finally, the narrator is at peace as she revives the "sounds of their voices" and the "parade of faces." Wilson uses the vernacular well here, like the term "doings." The familiar language makes this accessible and memorable.

Education: Jeanie Wilson graduated from Emporia High School in 1966. She received a B.S. in Education with English Emphasis (Emporia State University 1971) and an M.A. in English (University of Missouri-Kansas City 1991). **Career:** This poet published *Uncurling* (Mid-America Press 2000) and *The Door into the Dream*, co-authored with her husband Thomas Zvi Wilson (Mid-America Press 2006) The *Kansas City Star* listed *The Door into the Dream* as a noteworthy book, 2006. She has been a board member for The Writers Place in Kansas City and hosts The Writers Place Poetry Reading Series, which is co-sponsored by The Writers Place and the Johnson County Central Resource Library in Overland Park. She and her husband co-founded this series. She has worked in education administration at the University of Kansas and in Kansas City.

THE SCREEN PORCH

A wicker chair cradles me, rocks me to rhythms
of cicadas and crickets, bull frogs down at the pond.
Two whippoorwills cry around the house.
Night creeps in like a stain.

My great-great grandmother sat on this porch,
looked out across the fields, rested from the day's heat.
She has passed away along with my grandmother,
grandfather, and my aunt.

I am caught, tangled around by their doings,
their lives--a weaving of threads in the air of this house.
In the darkness, I listen to the sounds of their voices,
watch the parade of faces.

©2006 Jeanie Wilson "The Screen Porch," *The Door into the Dream.* ©2002 Denise Low photograph

DONALD WARREN LEVERING (1949 -)

Don Levering grew up in Kansas City, Kansas, and for many years has lived in Santa Fe. His poetry braids together myth and the natural world, but with uncertain logic and broken rhythms. As guest poet for the online Academy of American Poets forum, he described writing verse to be like a two-headed horse: "one wants rhythm, the other compression." This suggests the tension in his writing—the ongoing rhythm is studded with medallions of lightning-quick stories. His collaged images seem familiar, but they shift into illogical sequences.

The poem "Spider" suggests the urban myth of a person, perhaps his reader, waking up with a spider in his mouth. It also suggests the Southwestern Indigenous people's Spider Woman, who spins cosmic stories into realities. Just as this image of the "divine spider" becomes substantial, the poet turns himself into a marionette puppet, caught in strings pulled by an unseen puppeteer. The narrator is a helpless victim of a divorce, and then a victim of a larger web. The word "marrying" becomes another way of saying "entrapping."

The last part of the poem is a paradox, an unexpected twist. The shadows and dust and spider's spinning all continue despite personal tragedy of divorce. The narrator focuses on the spider's legs, mouth, and ability to spin silk—and he himself becomes spider-like, the singer of this poem.

Education: Don Levering was born and educated in Kansas City, Kansas. He received a B.A. in English (Baker University 1971), studied at the University of Kansas, and Lewis and Clark College, and then received an M.F.A. in Creative Writing from Bowling Green University (1978). **Career:** Levering's full-length books of poetry are *Outcroppings From Navajoland* (Navajo Community College Press 1985), *Horsetail* (Woodley Memorial Press 2003), and *Whose Body* (Sunstone Press 2007). He also has published poems in five chapbooks and many anthologies, journals, and online publications. Levering was a recipient of a National Endowment for the Arts Fellowship Grant in poetry, a finalist for the John Ciardi Prize, and first place winner in the Quest for Peace (rhetoric) Writing Contest.

SPIDER

To make a joyful sound,
just let the divine spider
climb out of your mouth
and go about its business
tying knots around your life.
So you're a marionette,
you still can feel yourself dancing
no matter who's pulling the strings.
Even as your divorce decree
is signed, the spider
goes on marrying you
to corners of household dust.
Eight legs, a ravenous mouth,
and the yen to spin silk in shadows.
Who wouldn't sing?

©2008 Donald Levering "Spider," *Whose Body* (Sunstone Press)

DENISE (DOTSON) LOW (1949 -)

As a fifth-generation Kansan, Denise Low-Weso writes verse that references the history and environmental concerns of this region. She grew up at the edge of Emporia, where the Flint Hills and town meet. Early experiences were with wildlife, grasslands plants, weather, and home gardens of the area. She learned to plant tomatoes every summer, and she learned early that nothing store-boughten can compare to their flavor. From William Allen White, William Stafford, and William S. Burroughs, she learned the variety of Midwestern experiences and the idioms of those literary traditions.

Like Stafford, Low is conscious of time as another dimension, which has its own cycles, more recursive than linear. Transformation, rather than static grief, characterizes this elegy to her mother, "Columbarium Garden." A "columbarium" is a cemetery for people who have been cremated. The poem is a study in contrasts: cold and sun; brick and ash; organic and mineral; sky and earth; animate and inanimate; grief and joy. These oppositions constantly shift.

Education: Denise Low earned B.A. and M.A. degrees in English (University of Kansas 1971, 1974) and an M.F.A. in Creative Writing from Wichita State University (1984). In 1997 she completed a Ph.D. at the University of Kansas in English. **Career:** Low has taught and been an administrator at Haskell Indian Nations University for 25 years. She also has been Visiting Professor at the University of Richmond and KU. She has written and edited more than 20 books of poetry and prose from BookMark-University of Missouri-Kansas City, Cottonwood-University of Kansas, Howling Dog, Mulberry, Woodley, Ice Cube, The Backwaters Press, and others. From 2007-2009 she served as Kansas Poet Laureate. She is a board member of the Associated Writers and Writing Programs. Her awards include recognition from the National Endowment for the Humanities, Lannan Foundation, Roberts Foundation, Kansas Arts Commission, and Poetry Society of America.

COLUMBARIUM GARDEN

Cold sun brings this mourning season to an end,
one year since my mother's death. Last winter thaw
my brother shoveled clay-dirt, she called it "gumbo,"
over powdery substance the crematorium sent us,
not her, but fine, lightened granules—all else
rendered into invisible elements. That handful
from the pouch, un-boxed, was tucked into plotted soil,
the churchyard columbarium, under a brass plaque
and brick retaining wall, as semblance of permanence.
Now my mother is a garden—lilies and chrysanthemums
feeding from that slight, dampened, decomposing ash.
Her voice stilled. One ruddy robin in the grass, dipping.

© 2007 Denise Low "Columbarium Garden" © 2007 Tim Janaake photograph

GARY J. LECHLITER (1951 -)

Gary Lechliter, born in Coffeyville, grew up in rural southeastern Kansas, where he sets many of his poems. He is an active reader, writer, editor, and supporter of literary arts in the Lawrence-Topeka area. He was the founder and editor of the literary magazine *I-70*, which featured authors who live along this interstate highway. His educational background is in psychology, and human quandaries appear in his verse. He also explores the varied dimensions of human imagination, collected in his book *Foggy Bottoms: Poems about Myths and Legends*. Known laws of reality are not enough for this poet, so he turns to confabulous tales.

The popular jackalope image, which I remember seeing in the 1950s, plays on the ignorance of Easterners about the grasslands. The fantastic animal is supposedly half antelope and half jack rabbit. This poem continues that legend by asserting "But I know she survives." The narrator has not seen this mythical creature, yet it has a presence drawn on postcards and ashtrays. Lechliter sets up his story, then shifts to first-person experience of being alone on "dusty backroads" and "railroad tracks," places that evoke solitude. In these wanderings, his jackalope becomes a female, despite her masculine rack of antlers. She hides, survives, and leaves behind an intangible aroma. How can she not be real?

Education: Gary Lechliter attended Neodesha High School; Pittsburg State University (B.A. in Psychology 1989); and the University of Missouri-Kansas City (M.A. in Psychology 1993). **Career:** Lechliter's books are *Under the Fool Moon* (Coal City Review Press 2001) and *Foggy Bottoms* (Coal City Review Press 2008). He has won the Langston Hughes and David Ray awards for poetry. He publishes poetry in many regional and national journals. Lechliter serves on the board of directors for Woodley Memorial Press at Washburn University. He lives in Lawrence and works as a Vocational Rehabilitation Specialist for the Veterans Administration Hospital in Topeka.

THE JACKALOPE

I have never seen
the crossbreed of legend
except in artwork,

postcards from Kansas,
ashtrays in roadhouses,
bars and malls.

But I know she survives
by hiding in brome,
scanning the flat land

for predators.
I have wandered alone
on dusty backroads

and railroad tracks,
smelling her stench
in the larkspur.

© 2008 Gary Lechliter, "The Jackalope," *Foggy Bottoms* (*Coal City Review* Press) © 2005 Denise Low photograph

SERINA ALLISON HEARN (1957 -)

Allison Hearn has been an active member of the poetry scene in Northeast Kansas for the last decade. She brings a traveler's experience to her writing, as she was born in Trinidad and is descended from Portuguese, Italian, African, British, and Chinese families. Besides her original home in Trinidad, she has lived in London, New York, Toronto, Princeton, and, since 1996, Lawrence. Her training is in art and design.

Hearn has written intermittently since she was a girl, she told a *Lawrence Journal World* reporter (2002), and she relates to the Kansas landscape because of its embodiment of time: "Kansas is the floor of an ancient sea." In her writings, she lives amidst sea stones, family stories, and Victorian houses, which she restores for a living. Hearn is a poet whose work connects to the real, historic world around her, and then it spins into imagined, hyperbolic (exaggerated) dimensions.

In "Yearly Restoration," an Ad Astra Poetry Contest winner, she delights in the names of commercial house paints: "Morning Mist," "Electric-Pink," "Evocative Sunlight," and "'Frosted-Hawthorn." These, as she paints, are her present-day layerings of experience over an 1850s frame house. So she participates in history, as she heals damage to "kicked-in doors." This renewal becomes its own shade, "Good-As-New." The narrator suggests stories like the "frat-boy parties" that recently ended and others, but most of all, this is a lyrical poem about sealing in the present, as though it could last through all years. The final word, "done," has finality, so that readers believe damage of the past is healed.

Education: Allison Hearn was born and raised in Trinidad, where she graduated from high school. She attended St Martin's School of Art, London. **Career:** Hearn has published poems in journals such as *Coal City Review, I-70* and others. She published *Dreaming the Bronze Girl* (Mid-America Press 2002), a Kansas City Star Notable Book, and a second book is ready for publication. She has worked as a writer, illustrator, and fashion designer in Trinidad and London. She writes poetry and renovates Victorian houses in Lawrence.

YEARLY RESTORATION

I bought a bucket of Morning-Mist
and painted the windows open.
Electric-Pink that splattered the floor
was patiently scraped with razor and rags
until the oak grain shone.
Evocative-Sunlight in multiple layers
hid the bruise marks on the walls.
Two emergency blankets of Ivory-Coast
tenderly covered, mended, kicked-in-doors.
Frosted-Hawthorn soothed in cross stitch brush strokes
graffiti etchings from drunken KU frat-boy parties.
The painted Victorian,
built by 1850s Lawrence-Kansas pioneers
stood, patiently, waiting for its wounds to heal.
Next morning I brought a gallon
of Good-As-New
and sealed the front porch done.

©2009 Serina Allison Hearn "Atlas of My Birth" ©2008 Denise Low, photograph

BRIAN DALDORPH (1958 -)

Brian Daldorph came to the University of Kansas English Department almost 20 years ago and has become a permanent resident of Kansas. He contributes to Kansas belles lettres in many ways: he writes; he organizes readings; and he is a writing class instructor at the Douglas County Jail—featured in *Poet's Market 2008*. He advocates for writers by publishing *Coal City Review*, a nationally recognized literary magazine. Daldorph's writing is marked by his awareness of social justice. He often uses the form of a dramatic monologue, where he assumes the voice of another character, to get inside human experience. In this way he is able to energize historic works.

"Last Word" is a sonnet that does not follow the pattern of a Shakespearean sonnet, yet some of the lines do rhyme; there are fourteen lines; and the ending is an unexpected reversal. This is a contemporary sonnet—it still has a lyric, emotional focus, yet it uses the sonnet form as a guideline, not a straitjacket. One of the enduring qualities of the sonnet form is its length, which sustains thought as long as most of us can concentrate. It fits the human mind like the length of a breath is gauged to our lung capacities. The speaker of this dramatic monologue is a writer. He believes God is counting his words, like breaths, from birth to death. As he writes late at night, he listens to night music of train whistles and be-bop jazz. "Yardbird" is a nickname for Charlie Parker.

For the speaker here, these sounds evoke thoughts of mortality. He may think that he will live forever, but in this poem he imagines his end as a single significant word, but which one? This prompts readers to ask the same question.

Education: Brian Daldorph was born and educated in Harrogate, Yorkshire, England. He received a B.A. (University of Kent 1983); M.A. (Illinois State University 1985) and Ph.D. in English (University of Illinois 1990). His dissertation topic was the poetry of W.S. Merwin. **Career:** Daldorph has taught English at the University of Kansas and in Japan, Senegal, and England. His books are *The Holocaust and Hiroshima: Poems* (Mid-America 1997); *Outcasts* (Mid-America 2000); *Senegal Blues* (219 Press 2004); and *From the Inside Out: Sonnets* (Woodley 2008). He publishes and edits *Coal City Review*.

LAST WORD

God knows the number of words I'll write.
God knows my first word
and He's been keeping score since then,
even when I'm up past midnight
listening to night trains and Yardbird,
trying to hold onto my heavy black pen.
Sometimes I think I could write forever,
just sit at my desk and not move
beyond the twitching of my hand. I'd not need a lover.
Words would be my picture-framed love.
Eventually there'd be only my last word left
to write. Perhaps I'd think about it for days,
stretched out on my death bed.
What should it be? Rain? Sea? Alone? Amaze?

© 2008 Brian Daldorph "Last Word," *From the Inside Out* (Woodley)

KATHLEEN JOHNSON (1959 -)

Kathleen Johnson has loved Kansas poetry for decades. This has led her to read widely, pursue an M.F.A. , and also to write reviews of regional and national poets. She wrote insightful, thorough reviews for the *Kansas City Star* for fifteen years. Now she edits the *New Mexico Review* in her new home of Santa Fe. Another aspect of her poetic skill set is her background in visual arts, with art history as an undergraduate major.

One of my own delights in poetry is visual images, and Johnson describes colors especially well. In "End of August," I enjoy the cat's "sapphire eyes," but the poet expands the image further to include "sharp points" and "all twilight." These detail the eyes as faceted, like a jewel, and dark, dark blue, like the evening sky. Other words that evoke colors are moon, sunflower, yellow, bluebirds, goldfinches, and black-eyed Susans. This spectrum of colors makes the poem more vivid.

"End of August" is a good landscape poem for students of poetry to read, because of the use of specifics—the plants are ragweed, candelaria, sunflowers, mulberry, and black-eyed Susans to emphasize season and well as sensual presence. This also illustrates how poets research specificity when writing. Good poets do as much fact checking as journalists. Exactly what birds, animals, and plants herald the end of summer? This poem is more than fine description and revival of a scene. The last line transforms details into a larger theme: survival.

Education: Kathleen Johnson graduated from Olathe High School and attended the University of Kansas for a B.F.A. in Art History (1985) and an M.F.A. in Creative Writing (2008). **Career:** Johnson's first book *Burn* (Woodley 2009) was a 2009 Kansas Notable Book. As a freelance book critic specializing in poetry, she published more than sixty book reviews in *The Kansas City Star* (2002-2009). Her *New Mexico Poetry Review* website is: http://newmexicopoetryreview.com/

END OF AUGUST

Tonight, while the half-moon hides
its dark side,
the Siamese tom stretches
black velvet paws,
claws splayed toward a dream:
he hunts, sapphire eyes
focused to sharp points,
all twilight
concentrated in his gaze.
Stealthy as a shadow, he curves
through a creek-bank jungle
of giant ragweed, candelaria,
sunflower stalks.
Yellow mulberry leaves litter the lawn.
From low branches,
bluebirds dive for insects.
Goldfinches search for seeds
in black-eyed Susans.
Baby cottontails munch in tall grass.
Quick eyes everywhere.

©2009 "End of August," *Burn* (Woodley) and photograph by Kathleen Johnson

CARYN MIRRIAM-GOLDBERG (1959 -)

One of the most active poets in Kansas is Lawrencian Caryn Mirriam-Goldberg, Kansas Poet Laureate 2009-2011. She conducts writing workshops and readings across the state. She teaches poetry to journal keepers, songwriters, lower income youth and adults, and cancer survivors. As a professor in a low-residency college, she also reaches students across the nation. Further, she is a founder of the transformative language arts curriculum, which promotes spoken and sung language as "a tool for personal and community transformation." She participates in international events and so has a global perspective on poem-making. Her poet laureate project is developing poetry workshop leaders, as well as public appearances.

Mirriam-Goldberg's verse plumbs the depths of consciousness. In "Spring Song" she situates the poem between waking and dream states. The poem also hovers between night and day; between winter and summer; and between imagination and reality. Sky, gravity, trees, birds, and stones are elements of nature—and so also are moments like sudden waking from a dream and love. The ending image of a stone, solid yet carrying an internal crack for years, is yet another paradox. What seems solid may shatter at any moment. This is fertile ground for the poet, as she explores the renewal of springtime.

Education: Caryn Mirriam-Goldberg was raised in Brooklyn and Manalapan, New Jersey. She received a B.A. in History from the University of Missouri (1985). At the University of Kansas she received an M.A. in Creative Writing (1988) and Ph.D. in English (1992). **Career:** Mirriam-Goldberg's books of poetry are *Landed* (Mammoth 2009), *Lot's Wife* (Woodley 2000); *Animals in the House* (Woodley 2004) and *Reading the Body* (Mammoth 2004). Her cancer memoir, *The Ground Begins at Your Feet* (Ice Cube 2009) has been favorably reviewed by *Library Journal* and others. Since 1996 she has been a professor at Goddard College in Vermont, working with the Individualized M.A. program. She founded and coordinated the Transformative Language Arts conference and Goddard's degree emphasis. She also has written books for teenagers, *Write Where You Are* and a biography of Sandra Cisneros.

SPRING SONG

What it is to wake at night not watered down
in overdrawn voices from the day, to see the space
and not figure in the space, to fall backwards
in a dream and realize it's a dream?
What waits, wet as fire, on the end of the line?
The rushing of wings, the billowing of thunderheads,
the crashing of car into lamp post, the slivering of bark
from tree, the waking suddenly for no reason?
Meanwhile, insects reproduce themselves like breath,
birds loosen the sky with flight,
stratus clouds streak across the moon,
kisses stop, and stones break apart
so easily that it's clear they've been cracked inside
for a long time. Each life a transference of water.
Each act just a way to move light around.
Even knowing this, why can't the heart stop asking?

© 2006 Caryn Mirriam-Goldberg "Spring Song," *Animals in the House* (Woodley)

BARRY ROBERT BARNES (1960 -)

Barry Barnes draws on the American-British poetic tradition and enlivens it each time he performs. Barnes can recite from memory poems by Langston Hughes, Robert Burns, and Shakespeare. He memorizes his own poems so performances can emphasize drama. This writer also appears on spoken word recordings, some of which improvise on Hughes's poetry. He writes about very contemporary themes, like Hughes, yet at the same time and on the same stage, he reaches back to previous centuries.

"Kicked to the Curb" is a rarity in American English verse: a successful social protest poem. The language is staccato, abbreviated sentences. Their brevity create emotional tension. As a performance poet, Barnes often uses drums with his spoken readings. The regular beat of this poem suggests the percussive accompaniment.

The straightforward dialect is made powerful by parallel yet varied comments. This is not necessarily an anti-war poem—the poet lists some plausible reasons for the conflict in the second stanza. The costs of war, nonetheless, are clear.

A political poem shares qualities with narrative poetry: embedded within these images is a storyline. Finally, this is a moral comment that protests the treatment of returning veterans, especially those with war wounds. The title has shock-effect, or hyperbole (exaggeration), to move readers to action.

Education: Barry Barnes is a life-long resident of Lawrence, where he attended public schools. **Career:** This poet's book of poetry, *We Sleep in a Burning House*, is from Mammoth Publications (2008). He adapted poetry of Langston Hughes to musical form for the audio CD *Plain and Simple Truth* (Chameleon Productions 2007). He appears with the Bopaphonics on these Chameleon spoken-word productions: *Let America Be America Again* (2006), *Channeling Langston* (2005), *P-Bop* (2004). *Super Cow* is another ensemble CD. His poems appear in the compilation *Kaw! Kaw! Kaw!* (Gonk Monster and Chameleon Productions 2000). Barnes produced CDs: *Blue in a Red State* (with Stacey Fox 2003) and *Straight Out of Kansas* (2005). He works for Hallmark in Lawrence and teaches zumba.

KICKED TO THE CURB

An army of amputees
returns from overseas.
Traumatic brain injuries:
can't hear, can't think,
can't speak, can't see,
post traumatic stress syndrome,
can't concentrate, can't eat, can't sleep.
Unexplained disorders and diseases
and what for?

What is the reason for this war?
Revenge for 9-11.
To free Iraqis.
War on terror.
Cheap oil.

When all our soldiers finally come home
will they be forgotten and kicked to the curb?

© 2008 Barry Barnes "Kicked to the Curb," *We Sleep in a Burning House* (Mammoth Publications)

ELIZABETH CAROLINE DODD (1962 -)

Elizabeth Dodd has lived in Kansas since 1989, when she became an English professor at Kansas State University. She publishes poetry and personal essays, and the natural world appears vividly in all her writings. She also publishes commentary on nature topics that are related to ecological issues, or ecocriticism. This is an emerging field of study in American belles lettres, one that has genesis in the 1930s writings of Nebraska author Loren Eiseley. The Flint Hills area of Manhattan often inspires her prose and verse, and from these she moves to human concerns.

This poem, "Lyric," begins with a question of faith. Bishop George Berkeley questioned materialism when he asked "If a tree falls in the forest and no one is around, does it make a sound?" Here, Dodd's scattering of "broken" bark and branches across snow create a "grammar" of affirmation. She includes the speaker of the poem—"I turn sideways"—as another natural element, not a dominator of wilderness, but rather one of many other "dark shapes." The poet's "hillside" consists of unseen realities, including song, the essence of lyrical poetry. Her verse transcends matter, and her answer to Bishop Berkeley is "Yes." She is outside logical paradigms, and in this new dimension, poetry is a sixth sense.

Education: Elizabeth Dodd received a B.A. in English and French from Ohio University in 1983; an M.F.A. in poetry from Indiana University in 1986; and a Ph.D. in American and British Literature from Indiana University in 1989. **Career:** Dodd has published two books of poetry: *Archetypal Light* (University of Nevada Press 2001) and *Like Memory, Caverns* (New York University Press 1992, Elmer Holmes Bobst Award). Her books of essays and criticism are *In the Mind's Eye: Essays Across the Animate World* (University of Nebraska Press, 2008), *Prospect: Journeys & Landscapes* (University of Utah Press, 2003, William Rockhill Nelson Award), and *The Veiled Mirror and the Woman Poet* (University of Missouri Press, 1992)'

LYRIC

It doesn't matter
whether
a tree falls
or doesn't on this hillside.
I am here
in this buoyant silence
lifting from snow cover.
There is no story to tell
about cause and effect,
no one to pull
the stiff sheet of grammar
over a scattered pattern
of bark and branches
broken on the snow.
I turn sideways
and the wind slips among us,
so many vertical,
dark shapes.

© 1992 Elizabeth Dodd "Lyric," *Like Memory, Caverns* (New York University Press).

WILLIAM SHELDON (1962 -)

William Sheldon was born in Fort Collins, Colorado, and moved from Montana to Kansas at the age of five. His father was an English professor at Emporia State University, so he has grown up with regional literary works, as well as immersion in this place's culture. Sheldon excels at the spare, emphatic stories of the western dialect. At the same time, as a professor's son, he learned British and American literary tradition from birth.

Sheldon's poems show that wisdom is the ultimate use of words, not momentary amusement. Each poem suggests, through character and metaphor, a method of understanding the larger world.

For example, blind Uncle Walt in "A Kind of Seeing" hears—or otherwise senses—a rattler while the narrator bales hay. Uncle Walt carries a stock cane instead of a white cane, and he uses it as a teaching tool. The blind man's feat of hearing a snake, though, is not the remarkable event of the poem. When the narrator wants to kill the venomous serpent, Uncle Walt says, "There's worse than snakes," and he lets the animal leave in peace. The uncle's language is understated, which emphasizes a calm stance in the face of threat. The nephew learns danger is the natural order of this cosmos, including the unspoken realm of human interactions. Yet revenge is not the appropriate response. Here Sheldon expounds a natural theology, based on lessons that arise in nature.

Education: Bill Sheldon received an M.F.A. from Wichita State University (Creative Writing 2006), where he studied with Albert Goldbarth; M.A. and B.S. in English, Emporia State University English (1986, 1984); and A.A. Dodge City Community College (1982). **Career:** Sheldon has worked as a carpenter's assistant, stage coach driver, bus station attendant, and journalist. For the last 17 years he has taught at Hutchinson Community College. His books are *Retrieving Old Bones* (Woodley 2002, Kansas City Star Noteworthy Book) and *Into Distant Grass* (chapbook *Midwest Quarterly* 2008). He has received a Kansas Arts Commission fellowship.

A KIND OF SEEING

Uncle Walt walked
the old Crook place
blinder than a rock,
swinging his stock cane
with spiteful accuracy
on the old cow
when she crowded
my lugging of the grain.
Or halted me with it
at the waist
 "Watch that wire"
before I felt its metal bite.
Once he hooked me
ass-end over appetite
from a half stack of bales,
and before my wind was back,
lifted coils
gently from the straw
and slid the diamondback
off into the whispering grass.
And to my "Kill it,"
his dusty voice,
"There's worse than snakes."

© 2002 William Sheldon "A Kind of Seeing," *Retrieving Old Bones* (Woodley)

AMY FLEURY (1970 -)

Amy Fleury was born and raised in Seneca, attended Kansas State University, and taught at Washburn University for more than ten years. She visited many area arts centers and colleges for readings and conferences. Her writing has a fresh quality, conveyed by a narrator who has a quiet excitement about the surroundings.

Even this elegy, "At Cather's Grave," which is set in a forest cemetery, has a brightness. Like Cather, the narrator is displaced from western plains. Monadnock in the poem is an isolated New Hampshire mountain that rises over pine forests, and it emphasizes the sense of shadow at the gravesite. The prairie skies become the contrasting life in the poem. The contrast of landscapes sets up an implicit irony in the poem, the plainswoman buried in a forest.

Fleury turns to landscape as eternity, like Cather' novels about the prairie create a literary heritage that continues. Fleury writes that "the prairie / is like a page," and so she joins the author with her own writings. She contrasts the dark New Hampshire woods with "sun-doused sedge" and also graveside and life. The last stanza integrates opposites with affirmation of the continuity of wind, which tells stories everywhere, and the land, which "will take us in," whether in forests or on the plains. Fleury herself recently moved to Louisiana, but will never truly leave Kansas.

Education: Amy Fleury graduated from Seneca High School. She received two English degrees from Kansas State University (B.S. 1991, M.A. 1994) and an M.F.A. in Creative Writing (McNeese State University, 1997). At K.S.U. she received the William H. Hickok Graduate Fellowship in Fiction.
Career: Fleury taught at Highland Community College (1997-1998), Washburn University (1998-2008), and McNeese State University, Lake Charles, Louisiana (2008 -). She received the Crab Orchard First Book Award for *Beautiful Trouble* (Southern Illinois University Press 2004), and she has a chapbook, *Reliquaries of the Lesser Saints* (RopeWalk Press, University of Southern Indiana 2008).

AT CATHER'S GRAVE

Veiled in deep New Hampshire pines,
you rest in a bed of mast and loam.
A pilgrim from the plains, I've come in homage
to your open-skied and earth-turned words.
Monadnock will not shadow you.

We both know that the prairie
is like a page, our living and dying
written in every tuck and swell.
I wish we could walk out together,
arms linked, toward the sun-doused sedge.

But everywhere, whether here
or there, the wind stories us
and the land will take us in.
We are all happy to be dissolved
into something so complete and great.

© 2004 "At Cather's Grave," Amy Fleury, *Beautiful Trouble,* Southern Illinois University Press

KEVIN YOUNG (1970 -)

Kevin Young, born in Nebraska, spent middle and high school years in Topeka before attending Harvard University. He is a professor at Emory University in Atlanta, where he also curates the Raymond Danowski Poetry Collection. As a poet he has won Guggenheim, National Endowment for the Arts, and Stegner Fellowships. When he was still a teenager, Thomas Fox Averill of Washburn sponsored Young to edit a book by Kansas University poet Edgar Wolfe, and he has been involved with writing, editing, teaching, and collecting poetry ever since.

Young's poetry begins with lean lines and sharp images. The poem "Childhood" appears to be spare, yet sensations build as a walk in the woods turns into a lifetime chronology.

This poem could be set in the Topeka area's Kaw River valley, where ash trees grow. The meditation on childhood begins with a "welcome" from the woods. He describes chicken-of-the-woods fungi on fallen trees, which seem to be listening ears. Beyond sight woodpeckers can be heard—which references John Keats' nightingale. The pivot in the poem comes before the halfway mark, with the question: "Where is nature human?" The narrator looks down from canopy heights to the ground, and the mood darkens. With the poem's nightfall, aging begins, and also a process of confusion. Young uses vivid comparisons to explain this mystery: strips of bark on the ground are a coded text. Darkness is like dangerous depths of water. In the last two lines is another shift, as mosquitoes bite: "Wish /them well. Wave." The poem tells us to embrace the dark.

Education: Kevin Young graduated from Topeka West High School. He has an A.B. in English and American Literature (Harvard University 1992) and M.F.A. in Creative Writing (Brown University 1996). **Career:** Young's books are *Most Way Home* (William Morrow 1995), National Poetry Series winner; *To Repel Ghosts* (Zoland Books 2001), finalist for the Academy of American Poets prize; *Jelly Roll: A Blues* (Alfred A. Knopf 2003), finalist for 2003 National Book Award in Poetry; *Black Maria* (Alfred A. Knopf 2005); and *Dear Darkness* (Alfred A. Knopf 2008). Young edits anthologies from Harper Perennial and Everyman. His poetry and essays have appeared widely in print & electronic media.

CHILDHOOD

Autumn & the leaves turn
to people—yellow, brown,
red—then die. Only ash
trees stay white, standing—

the woods welcome you, trail
like a tongue, half-hidden.
Ears cover fallen trees:
pale mushrooms, listening.

Stop & you can hear
the peckerwoods high up.
Where is nature
human? On the ground

bark thin & pale
as paper, coded Morse.
You are lost, path
unmarked. It grows

dark, you older, night
around you like a lake
you've swum out too far
into—tread moonlight

while the bugs begin
taking your blood
for their children. Wish
them well. Wave.

© 2008 "Childhood," Kevin Young, *Dear Darkness: Poems* (Alfred A. Knopf)

KEVIN JAMES RABAS (1974 -)

Kevin Rabas grew up in Shawnee, Johnson County. He attended area colleges and also Goddard in Vermont. Now he teaches creative writing at Emporia State University. He has a musical background, including training in marimba and other percussions. He still performs music regularly in eastern Kansas. While living in the Kansas City area, he developed talents as a jazz drummer, historian, and critic, which influence his poetry both in form and content. He writes about Charlie Parker ("Bird's Horn") and other musicians. He also approaches a poem like an improvised solo, with a musical phrase (like a poetic image) enunciated and then repeated in varying ways.

In the poem "Lightning's Bite," Rabas begins with a child's voice as a boy asserts that lightning is like a mammal with teeth. Throughout the poem, then, the narrator notices the sky in this new mode, or musical key. The clouds "look like they are carrying heavy sacks." The trees "wave" in the wind. And because this is a child's poem, imaginary "great dragons" can appear in the cloud formations. Next, the poem shifts back to an adult's perspective, or instrumental voice, as the narrator admits the phenomenon is simply wind. So the grown-up comforts the child. Yet the adult narrator is changed. When the storm passes, he sees wind as something more: "It is like standing under a bridge as a train goes over." The two perspectives merge into a third, as a musician would resolve a melody with a final chord.

Education: Kevin Rabas received a B.A. in English (University of Missouri-Kansas City, 1995); M.A. in English (Kansas State University, 1998); M.F.A. in Creative Writing (Goddard College, 2002); and Ph.D. in English (University of Kansas, 2007). **Career:** Rabas teaches at Emporia State University, where he co-directs the creative writing program and co-edits *Flint Hills Review*. His awards for poetry include the Langston Hughes Award. He has published *Bird's Horn* (Coal City Review Press 2007) and *Lisa's Flying Electric Piano* (Woodley 2009). His jazz poetry CD is *Last Road Trip*, with saxophonist Josh Sclar (http://kevinrabas.com/).

LIGHTNING'S BITE

Watch out. The lightning might come down
and bite you, my son says, and we look
to the gray, weighted clouds above us
that look like they are carrying heavy sacks
of hail or rain. Or snow, but it is too early for that.
So we hold out our hands and look for the droplets
that should come, and there are none.
So we look to the trees that wave and bend
and to the branches full of big green leaves,
branches that look like the necks of great dragons
twisting and fighting, when all this really is
is wind, and we go home, go inside, and watch
as the lights go out, and we listen to the storm above us.
It is like standing under a bridge as a train goes over.
But this train keeps coming, and rumbling, and my son
puts his hands over his ears. I take him in my arms,
and we do not tremble. We laugh.

© 2009 Kevin Rabas "Lightning's Bite," *Lisa's Flying Electric Piano* (Woodley)

CYRUS CONSOLE (1977 -)

Cyrus Console grew up in Topeka and currently studies creative writing in the University of Kansas doctoral program. He has worked as a metal worker and waiter as well as part-time instructor. His poetry returns to some of the oldest Anglo Saxon poetic traditions—delight in wordplay and riddles. He creates Rubik cubes made of his own subsets of vocabularies. Interlocking phrases suggest new structures, and readers enlarge their own vision by following Console's playful, inventive constructions.

In this selection from *Brief Under Water*, whose title refers to Kafka's *Brief an den Vater (Letter to His Father)*, Console connects mathematical progressions to language. He labels each section of this long sequence of prose poems with binary-based numbers. This poem (40 in the decimal system) appears to begin with a letter salutation, "dear Dad," informing him of a strong wind that rocked the "television antenna." The last sentence is like a bookend to that suggested narrative—the narrator ends the story with a box kite broken in that same wind. Shifts in perspective, specifically elevation, continue throughout. Also, each sentence builds on the one before, with words repeated and shifted into different parts of speech. The word "wind" (breeze) twists (or winds, with a long "i") throughout the poem's beginning. The original connection of the two meanings of "wind" converge. At the end of this prose poem, "broke" is a verb with connotations referencing weather, cover, and sun emerging from clouds. Then Console ends with both words in the final: "windbreak."

Education: Cyrus Console graduated from Topeka High School and attended the University of Kansas, where he received a B.S. in Organismal Biology (2000). He attended Bard College for the M.F.A. in Writing (2004). He works on a Ph.D. in the University of Kansas English Department. **Career:** Console's book *Brief Under Water* (Burning Deck 2008) is a collection of prose poems. He has won the Ana Damjanov Poetry Prize; Fund for Poetry Award; Victor Contoski Poetry Prize; and William Herbert Carruth Poetry Prize. He has published in *Boston Review, No: A Journal of the Arts, Critical Quarterly,* and *Lana Turner*. Recent readings include the Poetry Project at St. Mark's Church, Big Tent series in Lawrence, and the Holloway Series at the University of California, Berkeley.

BRIEF UNDER WATER: 10011

Dear dear, I put down, dear Dad, the great television antenna swayed in the wind. The meadow moved in long swathes under the wind. The wind swept the meadow around the cedars, as they were moss-grown rocks in a river of dry grass. In the wind the boys made a handsome tableau, their hair slanting vigorously from under their caps. The thick steel guys stood waves in the wind. Close by the anchors the wind came in towering chords. The wind fluted in the mouths of the gaping boys. Dead bees blew in the wind. Rain filled the sky. The rain pelted the rainwater, sheeting the meadow in incident light. The boys slowed at the line of trees. They walked into the trees. The trees surrounded the boys. The boys disappeared into the trees. The weather broke. The boys broke cover. The clouds broke up and the sun broke through. The box kite lay broken in a windbreak.

©2008 Cyrus Console, *Brief Under Water* (Burning Deck) © 2009 Paula Prisacaru photograph

BENJAMIN S. LERNER (1979 -)

Ben Lerner, from Topeka, studied poetry at Brown University. His writing is grounded in the 21st century—with all its nesting boxes of realities and simulations. In one poem he writes about a man watching himself on TV: "He watches the image of his watching the image on his portable TV on his portable TV." The occurrence of wordplay like this unifies Lerner's writings.

Lerner creates highly populated mappings of urban throughways. These include lifetime graphs, like Ronald Reagan's biography. Such a person's identity is reduced to an icon—the movie star president—and so human experience is easily commodified. Lerner told a *Jacket* magazine interviewer that he is concerned with "commercialization of public space and speech."

Another of Lerner's concerns is extended poems with variations on a theme, such as his first book, *The Lichtenberg Figures*. This interest extends to prose poem sections of *Angle of Yaw*, a 2007 Kansas Notable Book and National Book Award nominee. Here, Lerner also shows interest in technologically expanded sight. The term "angle of yaw" is a physics term for the tiny sideways shiftings of an object like a bullet or airplane as it moves forward through its line of travel. This only can be observed from perspective of great distance, possible through optical aids. The poet, then, becomes a voyeur with infinite personal interactions to sort. He lives in not the classical age of art nor the modern nor postmodern. His is a land of fast, flattened social interactions, a hyper-industrial age where any human experience, not just labor, can be sold on E-bay.

This prose poem objectively classifies contemporary art forms. The narrator defines art in relationship to its public context. The poem progresses from static genres, painting and sculpture, to more dynamic ones. The dictionary-like tone reinforces the theme of art's isolation.

Education: Ben Lerner graduated from Topeka High School. He attended Brown University (B.A. Political Theory 2001), and earned an M.F.A. in Poetry (2003). **Career:** Lerner's books are from Copper Canyon Press: *The Lichtenberg Figures* (2004, Hayden Carruth Prize) and *Angle of Yaw* (2006), nominated for a National Book Award. He is professor at the University of Pittsburgh writing program. He edits *No: A Journal of the Arts*.

from *ANGLE OF YAW*

If it hangs from the wall, it's a painting. If it rests on the floor, it's a sculpture. If it's very big or very small, it's conceptual. If it forms part of the wall, if it forms part of the floor, it's architecture. If you have to buy a ticket, it's modern. If you are already inside it and you have to pay to get out of it, it's more modern. If you can be inside it without paying, it's a trap. If it moves, it's outmoded. If you have to look up, it's religious. If you have to look down, it's realistic. If it's been sold, it's site-specific. If, in order to see it, you have to pass through a metal detector, it's public.

©2006 Ben Lerner *Angle of Yaw* (Copper Canyon)

Ad Astra Poetry Writing Guide: Prompts

By Caryn Mirriam-Goldberg

The old saying is that amateur writers borrow but great writers steal, yet to be fair, if you use any line or inspiration from another writer's poem, be sure to give credit to that writer. You can do this by simply having a footnote to the poem or an asterisk next to the title that connects to a sentence like, "Inspired by. . ." or "Thanks to. . . for the
line. . . ."

*(1902) **Langston Hughes:*** After reading this poem aloud, use the line "I've known rivers," and write until you can say no more. Then repeat "I've known rivers" and launch another direction. Keep going until you've said everything you can about rivers. Or focus on one river you've known well, first writing a list of all your stories about that river (or experiences you had that involved the river), and then plucking one story off your list, and writing that story. Another option is to make a list-poem of all the vivid moments you experienced at this river.

*(1912) **Gordon Parks:*** Write about the funeral or memorial service of someone who has influenced you, focusing on how the event itself showed you something new and vital. You can also write about what you experienced at the funeral of a loved one, finding images to convey the weight and depth of your feelings to show the magnitude of loss. You can instead focus especially on a line that particularly speaks to you, such as "After many snows I was home again" or "Time had whittled down to mere hills the great mountains/ of my childhood," and then use the line that grabs you most as the title or first line of your poem. Or write of someone or something that seemed so large and of such great importance when you were a child, and how it seems to you now.

*(1914) **William Stafford:*** Write a poem as a letter to a distant friend. Or using the line, "You can watch/ the land by the hour," look at a particular place once an hour and write a line of what you see until you have an hourly-focused poem. You can also take the line, "Yes. Though there's wind in the world," and use it as a diving board into your own poem (wherever the line and the wind takes you).

(1924) Jack DeWerff: After reading "Married to a Cowboy," begin your own writing with the phrase, "It's ain't easy being...." or "It isn't easy being..." and write what follows for you. Or whimsically or ruggedly write you own, "Married to a Cowboy," and see what comes.

(1931) Thomas Zvi Wilson: Write a poem that uses the notion of the moon surrendering, or write of the wind as a person (sleeping, snoring, waking or whatever else it's doing). You could also begin a poem with the line, "I count my sins on the porch," and see where such counting and writing leads you.

(1932) William Kloefkorn: Take a historic figure (like Carry A. Nation, or even Carry as a private person) and have him/her come into your house and wreak havoc. Or take an old song, such as the "LTL," and wind a poem around it and its history.

(1935) Jo McDougall: Write your own blessing poem, or write a blessing poem specifically for someone who could use an ordinary or unusual gift (such as a dryer). Or write about hanging clothes to dry, and see where the line leads you.

(1935) Charles Plymell: Title something, "Not a Regular Kansas Sermon" or a variation ("Not a Regular Kansas Love Song" or "Not a Regular Kansas Day") and write. Or start with the words, "Your grandmother" (or "grandfather") and go from there. Or use the sentence starter, "I've yet to see...." and fill in the blanks.

(1936) Kenneth Irby: Begin a poem with the word "In" to show a particular setting. Or use a phrase such as "a real dog and pony show" to get started with writing wherever you're led. Or use the phrase, "astronomical agility," in the middle of a poem to start new language.

(1936) Gloria Vando: Write about having "....never know myself/ as..." and fill in the blanks. Or take the idea of thriving on luck, and write a poem about what that could mean, in specific images and details, to your life. Or write about a loss in your life that has actually brought you new insights and new luck even.

(1936) Victor Contoski: Take a fairy tale, such as "Jack and the Beanstalk," and set it down in Kansas somewhere to write what happens. Or use the sun going down as a background image in a poem. You can also try writing a poem where you repeat a word, such as "rocking rocking the cradle in its branches" to show the action even more acutely in your language.

(1936) Elizabeth Schultz: Write a poem with very short lines, such as Schultz's "Watching the Kansas River." Or write of something you see in the earth and sky as if it's a pattern or design. Or simply go to your local river, and write what you see.

(1940) Harley Elliott: Consider Elliott's "Butterfly Master," and then write a poem or story focusing on one small being or thing you watch carefully, such as a bumblebee, small pebble in the garden, or spool of thread. Or take the line, "We rush together/ earth and sky," use it as scaffolding to start your own poem. Or write about "the shining light of its face" when describing something.

(1941) Robert Day: Day takes an activity that lasts one day, sunrise to sunset. Write a day-long poem. Or write a memory poem about a childhood event from your adult point-of-view.

(1941) Diane Glancy: Glancy describes the impermanence of the world in "Indian Summer." After reading this poem, describe something or some place you pass by regularly, with an eye toward how it's always in motion. Or take a line from her poem and use it to jump-start your own writing. Or use the line, "The world is at a loss and I am part of it" to write about what these words mean to you.

(1941) Billy Joe Harris: Write about your life as a bridge between past and
present or one generation and another or one place and another. Perhaps you may want to take a legend from around the world and build a poem around it.

(1941) Jonathan Holden: Start your own writing with the line, "There is no minor league for birds" and keep writing to see what you discover. Or write about a night game of any kind you envision. Or take the line, "To stay alive/ out in the field, you must..." and see where continuing that line leads you.

(1941) Michael L. Johnson: Write about your "own uncertain ghosts," describing whatever haunts you in life. Or using the line, "Things are different out here," jump into your own writing about

how things can be different. Or write about what it means to "remember so deep."

(1941) Jim McCrary: Write a poem a day to see where it gets you. Or write about how the clouds "gather/ push east and south/ to here." Or describe something by its motion. You can also make a list of images that describes aspects of clouds you have seen or imagine you will see.

(1941) B.H. Fairchild: After reading "Hearing Parker for the First Time," put on some music that means a great deal to you, and write about what images you hear in the song. Or listen to something completely new for the first time, and describe it in images and rhythms.

(1943) Steven Hind: After reading "Great Blue Heron," write of a moment you experienced under "the gravel of stars" or during any very starry night. Or write of sightings of great blue herons (as a list poem or as a description of one particular sighting).

(1943) Phillip Miller: Write about your body as a tree, or take a line from Miller's poem to begin your own writing about your body or another body. Or write about how "the body owns us." Or you can describe the body as a field, a sky, a patch of tulips, or whatever else you want.

(1943) James Tate: Write something about late harvest—either the literal harvest in the fields and gardens around you or what you're harvesting in your life or both. Or begin a poem with, "I look up and see…"

(1944) Stephen Meats: Write something titled, "My Advice" or "Your Advice." Or write of a journey on "any rocked road" to find more than just the scenery. Or use the line, "For once, stop/ and get out of the car" as a starting point.

(1944) Patricia Traxler: Write a poem about waiting. Or write about "another night," focusing on the repetition of something that comes and what the story behind that story is.

(1945) Jeanine Hathaway: Using the term, "Reconnaissance," write of a mission of some sort that happens in an unlikely setting (such as in a home before dawn). Or write about "the unsettling grace of morning." You can also write about dwelling in "the immense heartbeat" of your own atmosphere.

(1945) Michael Poage: Write of the moon as a part of us (such as "a human back"). Or focus a poem on "home's street," opening your eyes to what's there (or "home's road" if you live in the country). Write a poem about a bird, the air, or the moon (or all three).

(1945) Judith Roitman: Describe something or a moment in time sideways by focusing on what you might see out of the corner of your eyes. Or write about the motion of a leaf falling, or something else moving, freeing yourself to use images that might not initially make sense to find a new kind of sense.

(1947) John Moritz: Write your own homage to a Midwestern city, focusing on specific moments and images, such as "while waiting to be seated/ a gar circles a ceramic pond counterclockwise."

(1947) Patricia Reeves: Write of something you or others experienced as a chronology (time sequence).

(1948) Linda Rodriguez: "Coyote Invades Your Dreams" is one way of bringing together the mythic and the real. Write your own piece on "_____ (fill in the blank) Invades My Dreams," using something you dream of often as the invader.

(1948) Albert Goldbarth: Begin with the phrase, "I always wondered why they called...." and then land on something's name that you wonder about, or write about a moment the land seemed "enameled."

(1948) Jeanie Wilson: Write about ways the night can come (as in "Night creeps in like a stain"). Or write of a porch and the stories it has held for you.

(1949) Donald Levering: Beginning with the phrase, "To make a joyful sound," start writing. Or describe a spider in great detail and what the description mirrors about life beyond the spider.

(1949) Denise Low: Describe your life, or the life of someone you love (still alive or passed on) as a garden. Or focus on "one ruddy robin in the grass" or another singular creature and write of what watching it shows you of life.

(1951) Gary Lechliter: After reading "The Jackalope," write your own piece called "A Kansas Postcard" (or another state) and describe something real or mythical you might put out there to the world to show them a new angle of a place.

(1957) Serina Allison Hearn: If you were to create a set of paints for your house (or memory), what would you name the colors? You can look at Hearn's choices as a starting point, and then write a poem using your own palette. Or write about a house, or part of a house, that might need repair.

(1958) Brian Daldorph: Taking the last line of Daldorph's poem "Last Word," – "What should it be? *Rain? Sea? Alone? Amaze?*" – as the first line of what you'll write, land on last words for your life, or for a part of your life that is now ending (e.g. last child grows up and leaves home, retirement, etc.), write your own last words.

(1959) Kathleen Johnson: Write about the end of August, often a yearned for ending time in Kansas because of the heat. Or write about a moment when the moon seems to hide, paying close attention to what you can see, hear, smell, or touch in the dark.

(1959) Caryn Mirriam-Goldberg: In Mirriam-Goldberg's "Spring Song," she asks at the poem's end, "Even knowing this, why can't the heart stop asking?" Answer the question she poses about how, even knowing the spirit and vitality of everything, why we still long for more. Or write your own poem composed of questions instead of answers.

(1960) Barry Barnes: Write a poem specifically focused on what veterans or other marginalized people might face. Or use the word "Can't...." to begin a description of someone, some place or something.

(1962) Elizabeth Dodd: After reading Dodd's "Lyric," write of a moment being alone outside, focusing on the shapes of what you see and experience. Or write of what you can see in a moment that's especially vertical.

(1962) William Sheldon: Write something focused on "a kind of seeing." Or write a poem as homage to a relative, friend or town character.

(1970) Amy Fleury: Write of a moment when you were "....happy to be dissolved/ into something so complete and great." Or write of the prairie "like a page."

(1970) Kevin Young: Make a list of moments and items that represent your childhood to you, and then link them together in a piece of writing. Or using the line "Stop & you can hear...," write about what you can hear when you stop.

(1974) Kevin Rabas: After reading "Lightning's Bite," write about a moment you witnessed lightning—alone or with others—that stands out for you. Or write a series of small paragraphs or stanzas about moments of lightning.

(1977) Cyrus Console: After reading Console's poem, write your own description of a moment by conveying a panoramic view of much that's happening at that moment. Aim for short lines and few adjectives, if any. Or take a phrase from this poem, such as "Dead bees blew in the wind," and use it to start your own writing.

(1979) Benjamin J. Lerner: Using the logic of this poem's language, try out "if it...., it's a...." to describe what's around you. Or take one of Lerner's sentences as the title of your own writing, and see what
you can create when you write something called, for example, "If you have to look down, it's realistic

AUTHOR INDEX

Barnes, Barry 86-87
Console, Cyrus 98-99
Contoski, Victor 26-27
Daldorph, Brian 80-81
Day, Robert 32-33
DeWerff, Jack 12-13
Dodd, Elizabeth 88-89
Elliott, Harley 30-31
Fairchild, B.F. 42-43
Fleury, Amy 92-93
Glancy, Diane 34-35
Goldbarth, Albert 68-69
Harris, Billy Joe 44-45
Hathaway, Jeanine 56-57
Hearn, Allison Serina 78-79
Hind, Steven 46-47
Holden, Jonathan 36-37
Hughes, Langston 6-7
Irby, Kenneth 22-23
Johnson, Kathleene 82-83
Johnson, Michael L. 38-39
Kloefkorn, William 16-17
Lechliter, Gary 76-77
Lerner, Ben 100-101

Levering, Donald 72-73
Low, Denise 74-75
McCrary, Jim 40-41
McDougall, Jo 18-19
Meats, Stephen 52-53
Miller, Phil 48-49
Mirriam-Goldberg, Caryn 84-85
Mortiz, John 62-63
Parks, Gordon 8-9
Plymell, Charles 20-21
Poage, Michael 58-59
Rabas, Kevin 96-97
Reeves, Trish 64-65
Rodriguez, Linda 66-67
Roitman, Judith 60-61
Schultz, Elizabeth 28-29
Sheldon, Bill 90-91
Stafford, William 10-11
Tate, James 50-51
Traxler, Patricia 54-55
Vando, Gloria 24-25
Wilson, Jeanie 70-71
Wilson, Thomas Zvi 14-14
Young, Kevin 94-95

Denise Low, 2007-2009 Kansas Poet Laureate, has been writing, reviewing, editing and publishing literary and scholarly articles for 30 years. She is the author of ten collections of poetry and six books of essays, including a biography of Langston Hughes (co-authored with husband Thomas Pecore Weso). In addition, she has edited anthologies related to literature, ecological matters, and Laguna author Leslie Marmon Silko. Her writing appears in North American Review, Midwest Quarterly, S. Connecticut Review, Chariton Review, Coal City Review and many others. She has been a faculty member and administrator at Haskell Indian Nations University; and visiting full professor at the University of Kansas (2008) and University of Richmond (2005). She serves as vice president and conference chair of the Associated Writers and Writing Programs Association. Awards and fellowships are from the National Endowment for the Humanities, Lannan Foundation, Poetry Society of America, and Roberts Foundation. Her sites are http://deniselow.blogspot.com and www.deniselow.com

Caryn Mirriam-Goldberg is 2009-2011 Kansas Poet Laureate. As a poet, writer, teacher and facilitator, Caryn explores and celebrates how the spoken, written and sung word can inspire lives and communities. She is founder of Transformative Language Arts at Goddard College, where she teaches. Caryn's the author or editor of ten books and a long-time writing workshop facilitator and performer. She has engaged writers from communities of low-income housing, American Indian, cancer survivors, and environmental groups. Writing, telling stories and listening to one another is part of the work of Tikkum Olam, the Hebrew phrase that means putting back together the broken world. Her website is www.carynmirriamgoldberg.com.